DEMOCRACY AND NORTH AMERICA

DEMOCRACY AND NORTH AMERICA

edited by

ALAN WARE

FRANK CASS

LONDON • PORTLAND, OR

First published in 1996 in Great Britain by
FRANK CASS & CO. LTD.
900 Eastern Avenue, London IG2 7HH

and in the United States of America by
FRANK CASS
c/o ISBS
5804 N.E. Hassalo Street
Portland, Oregon 97213-3644

Transferred to Digital Printing 2004

British Library Cataloguing in Publication Data
A catalogue record for this book is available from the British Library

ISBN 0 7146 4717 9 (hardback)

0-7146 4264 9 (paperback)

Library of Congress Cataloging-in-Publication Data

This group of studies first appeared in a Special Issue:
'Demcoracy and North America' of *Democratization,* Vol.3,
No.1, Spring 1996, published by Frank Cass and Company
Limited.

Typeset by Frank Cass & Co. Ltd.

Contents

Introduction   **Alan Ware**   1

Constitutional Angst: Does American
Democracy Work?   **Nelson W. Polsby**   11

The Poverty of Canadian Politics?   **Gordon T. Stewart**   28

Democracy in Mexico   **George Philip**   46

The Segregated State? Black Americans and
the Federal Government   **Desmond King**   65

Democracy and the Reconstitution of Canada   **Ines C. Molinaro**   93

The Messenger as Policy-Maker:
Thinking About the Press and Policy
Networks in the Washington Community   **Adrienne M. Jamieson**   114

Direct Democracy in California:
Example or Warning?   **Wyn Grant**   133

Notes on Contributors   150

Introduction

ALAN WARE

The essays in this volume are about democracy in North America. The three countries in continental North America – Canada, the United States and Mexico – have had widely differing experiences in their attempts to democratize. Moreover, in the two countries that did so successfully, Canada and the United States, the democratic institutions have worked in very different ways. Each of the essays that follow focuses on one of the countries and examines aspects of the particular process of democratization, or on the debates that have surrounded the democratic institutions that were established, or on the working of political institutions that in some way are especially associated with the North American democratic experience.

Democratization in North America

The United States was the first country in the world to democratize. A mass white, adult male franchise became established during the 1830s. Before that decade the United States was a kind of halfway house between a wholly elite dominated regime and a democratic one; as Silbey notes, a

> centrepiece of the emerging postconstitutional political nation was its political leadership. As in the colonial era, the general population continued to accept the social elites as the natural leaders of the community. Accorded, as before, an uncoerced deference from below, they were generally the men elected to office; they ran politics at every level, their role and place secure.[1]

The extension of the franchise in the 1830s, and the rapid growth of competitive political parties in that decade, created a popular input into politics. From then, American democracy was to be characterized by a tension between the pressures coming from below and the need to impose some kind of order from the centre. Perhaps more than in any other democratic country the pressures from below for a say in the decisions of government created difficulties for political elites in providing effective government.

In part, this tension originated in the constitutional arrangements that had been established 50 years earlier. The men who had gathered at the Constitutional Convention in Philadelphia in 1787 were not democrats.

However, while they did not look back to the democracy of ancient Athens, both directly and indirectly they did look back to the model of the Roman republic.[2] In doing so, they were worried just as much about the concentration of power in government as they were that the popular input into government might be so great that politics would become a lever through which the many would undermine social relations that had been founded on property rights. To that end, they devised political institutions that would frustrate the concentration of power. In 1787 the individual states did not merge their identity into a single unitary state, but rather they became linked to each other through federalism; three separate branches of government, each with distinctive procedures for electing or selecting their members were created; these three branches had a variety of powers that served to check or balance other branches. Consequently, one of the most unusual features of American democratization was that it developed in the context of political institutions that were highly decentralized and fragmented.

This decentralization has prompted persistent debates about whether American democracy actually works, and, if it does not, whether and how it can be made to work better. Municipal reformers in the late nineteenth century, the Progressives at the beginning of the twentieth century, party government advocates in 1950, and more recently many others have claimed that there are serious flaws in American democratic government. Some have asserted that what has emerged is not especially democratic, others have argued that it provides for inefficient government, and there are those who make both of these claims. But by no means all commentators have taken this line. In an era when the literature on the effectiveness of American democracy seems to have mushroomed, Nelson W. Polsby's essay in this volume, 'Constitutional Angst: Does American Democracy Work?', places America's democratic record in context.

There might appear to be one obvious parallel between Canada's path to democracy and that of the United States. Both countries established representative political institutions based on a franchise that was extended to a majority of adult males before the industrial and financial sectors of the economy had become more important than the primary sectors. However, although it has some significance, this point cannot be pushed that far. While Canada's primary economy was dominant until well into the twentieth century, it was not until after the First World War that virtually all males obtained the vote. Between 1867 and the 1914–18 war between about 60 and 90 per cent of males were enfranchised – variations between provinces were considerable.[3] Consequently, the situation pre-1918 was perhaps more like that in the pre-1830s United States than in the post-1830s American era – political elites had to compete for the vote, but significant portions of the male population, as well as all women, were excluded from the electorate.[4]

Nevertheless, the common experience of mass enfranchisement before industrialization did have at least one important consequence for both countries: the drive for democracy was not associated, as it was in many European countries, with the mobilization of the urban working class. In turn, this was to affect the nature of the party systems that developed, particularly in relation to problems posed for socialist parties seeking to organize in working class communities. This consideration aside, the experience of the two countries is very different. In Canada representative institutions came with the uniting of the remaining British colonies in continental North America in 1867.[5] The potential military threat from south of the border, where there was a huge army immediately following the Civil War, prompted the British government and the socio-political elites in the colonies to come up with a solution that had eluded them earlier. And that solution focused on the provision of effective government. Thus while American democratization had occurred in the context of a widespread concern by elites to disperse power, in the Canadian case the prime movers of the constitution wanted power to be concentrated.

Canada was created as a federal system, but the federal government was granted such wide-ranging powers that, even as late as the 1950s, commentators could describe it as quasi-federal. (Nevertheless, by that time changes were already under way that would transform the relationship between the federal government and the provinces, and which eventually would make the American system appear rather centralized by comparison.) After 1867 Canada came to be ruled by a coalition of socio-economic elites in Ontario and Quebec. Quebec was a socially conservative province whose political leaders were able to keep control of their largely passive voters and who could use this as a resource for cutting deals with their Ontarian counterparts. Within government power accumulated in the hands of chief ministers – the premiers in the provinces and, most especially, the prime minister at the federal level. The source of prime ministerial power in the late nineteenth century and early twentieth century was patronage. More than in any other Westminster-style democracy, and certainly far more than was ever possible in the United States, extensive patronage resources were concentrated in one officeholder.[6]

For more than 80 years this centralized form of representative democracy provided a stable solution to the problem of how to govern a large country containing a territorially-based minority sub-culture that constituted about one-quarter of the population. One of the challenges to that solution came from rapid change in French Canadian society. The so-called 'quiet revolution' that Quebec underwent in the 1950s and 1960s turned a religious, socially conservative population into a secular and liberal one. This transformation in the province, from a largely non-democratic to a democratic political culture, would surely have forced change in the polity anyway. But at the same time as it was occurring political institutions were also being re-created. Part of the groundwork for this had been laid decades earlier by decisions of the Judicial Committee of the Privy Council in Britain, Canada's final court of appeal until 1949, which from the late nineteenth century had struck down many of the powers to intervene in the economy that the federal government supposedly possessed in the 1867 constitution. Furthermore, from the 1960s, successive federal governments started to transfer powers away from itself to the provinces in order to resolve conflicts between them. By the 1970s Canada had moved from a 'quasi federal' to a 'bottom heavy' form of federalism. In his essay, 'The Poverty of Canadian Politics?', Gordon T. Stewart explains the role played by political leadership in Canada, and the methods available to leaders, in both the formation of Canadian democracy and in its transformation in recent decades.

Unlike the two other countries, Mexico has not democratized. Moreover, this failure cannot be explained away simply as the result of its having a less developed economy than the two states to its north. Even when it is compared with the mineral exporting countries of South America its record is peculiar; Reuschemeyer et al. describe it as 'a case whose democratic record is clearly below what one would expect on the basis of the country's level of development'.[7] The Revolution of 1910–17 resulted neither in the creation of representative democratic institutions nor immediately in the centralization of power. It was an example of a political system with elections but without democracy. After 1929, however, there were significant institutional developments that were to facilitate the long term persistence of a mainly non-repressive authoritarian regime. Socio-political institutions were created that enabled important sectors of society and economy, including labour, to be co-opted by the ruling party. The interests of subordinate classes and groups were, at least to some extent, catered for by a party that held elections but which would not hesitate to rig them when that was necessary. However, some opposition parties were not only tolerated, but actually encouraged to form, by the Institutional Revolutionary Party (PRI), as it was called after 1946, to focus attention on its own indispensability. The dynamics of this stable regime, and the more recent pressures on it to democratize, are explicated in George Philip's essay, 'Democracy in Mexico'.

Democratic Institutions in North America

The failure of Mexico to democratize should not blind us to the problems in the democratic institutions and practices of the two other countries. In the

United States the most important limitation in the scope of democracy has been with respect to the role of black people in American society. The democracy that was established in the 1830s was one that quite explicitly excluded the vast majority of black people – people who were slaves – because the legal existence of slavery was acknowledged in the 1787 Constitution. The Civil War freed and enfranchised African-Americans, but within thirty years southern states had enacted Jim Crow laws that removed many of their civil rights and imposed segregation in most areas of life. The US Supreme Court's decision in *Plessy v. Ferguson (1896)* confirmed the rights of southern states to impose racial segregation if they chose to. While the judicial decisions and legislation of the 1950s and 1960s subsequently removed the legal barriers to black participation in American political society, the position of African-Americans in that society remains problematic. They continue to be disproportionately 'over-represented' at the bottom of the economic ladder, and since the late 1970s courts have increasingly been restricting the use of affirmative action programmes designed to create greater opportunities for the economic advancement of black people. After the 1994 elections, both state legislatures and the US Congress have been arenas in which Republican politicians have sought to eliminate such policies.

Until recently, however, it has been widely assumed that the failure to include black people within the American democratic polity was simply a problem caused by the South, on the one hand, and by the fragmentation of political power within a federal system, on the other. It was the southern states that had maintained slavery and it was the southern states that had enacted the Jim Crow laws. It was an unfortunate consequence of the decentralization of power in the US political system that political elites in the rest of the country could do little to prevent this. However, as Desmond King's essay, 'The Segregated State?' shows, after 1912 the federal government itself started to practise segregation; it was not until the 1940s that the dismantling of this system began. This experience has important implications for our understanding of American democratic institutions. The question 'who is included in the polity?' has always been controversial throughout American political history because a significant portion of those included have wanted to exclude others. While, of course, there is far less opposition today about the formal political rights of African-Americans, a new group, illegal immigrants from Mexico and the countries to its south (and their children), has emerged as the object of political exclusion. In the 1990s there has been a growing demand in the western states for these people to be denied access to all public resources, including education and social services. American democracy has always contained strains of liberalism and illiberalism, and it is clear that the former has never triumphed completely.

In Canada, the 'question of who is included in the polity' has been less controversial. The issue of the rights of Native Americans has prompted less political backlash, for example, than it has in the United States. This is not to say, though, that the terms on which different groups are included in the Canadian polity has not been the subject of dispute. As Kymlicka notes, 'Many of the pivotal moments in Canadian history have centred on ... attempts to renegotiate the terms of federation between English, French, and Aboriginals'.[8] Especially since the breakdown of the old elite-based system, the central problem of Canadian democracy has become 'how are the different social groups to be linked to each other?'. The difficulties of operating an increasingly 'bottom heavy' form of federalism, were compounded by the decision of Liberal prime minister Pierre Trudeau to repatriate the Canadian constitution in 1982. This was achieved despite the opposition of Quebec, and since then efforts to complete the re-designing of the constitutional arrangements – first in the Meech Lake agreement and then in the Charlottetown accord have failed. Following the 1992 referendum, in which the Charlottetown accord was rejected, and the 1994 election in which two anti-Ottawa parties became the second and third largest parties in the federal parliament, Canada seemed to be a democratic country in danger of disintegrating. In her essay in this volume, 'Democracy and the Reconstitution of Canada', Ines C. Molinaro considers Canada's experience in seeking to redraw its constitutional arrangements in a way that will facilitate both consent from, and equality among, its citizens.

As I suggested earlier, one of the principal differences between Canada and the United States was that from the time when parties started to compete for the votes of mass electorates there has been pressure 'from below' in America. American mass opinion and sentiment has not always been easy to channel. It might be tempting to argue that a free press, founded on constitutional guarantees of free speech, contributed to the problem of managing popular demands from the beginning of the democratic era. But this was not the case. For much of the nineteenth century most newspapers were tied to one party or the other not by mere sentiment but by financial necessity. They were small, local enterprises and were dependent on the official advertisements that local governments could put their way; in many instances they were one-person operations. It was not until the last quarter of the century that independent journalism became more prevalent. In part this was made possible by mergers and consolidation.[9]

By the twentieth century the press had become a major political actor, or rather set of actors, in its own right, first at the local and state level and later at the national level. Franklin Roosevelt's transformation of the role of the federal government was a key factor in bringing this about, and the advent of radio, and later television, further contributed to the growing power of the press. In virtually no other democracy is the press as unconstrained by the state as it is in the US. In her essay, 'The Messenger as Policy Maker', Adrienne Jamieson explains how the so-called 'fourth branch' of government interacts with the other three.

In spite of the concentration of power at particular periods – for example, in the hands of the parties in the late nineteenth century – what might be called the spirit of democracy, that power should rest with the people, has consistently resurfaced in America and prompted demands that the political system be reformed to ensure that power does reside there. At the beginning of the twentieth century politicians and activists in the Progressive movement advocated a variety of institutional reforms, including the replacement of bureaucracies founded on the spoils systems with ones run by professional administrators. Many of these reforms were enacted, especially in the western states. Then at the end of the 1960s and the 1970s there were successful demands for the reform of presidential nominating procedures and campaign finance laws. And in the 1990s further reforms have been enacted including, in several states, term limits on state legislators. One of the most interesting instruments of popular control advocated by the Progressives was the initiative referendum. Several European countries have provisions for referendums, and it is a device that is used extensively in Switzerland. But the significance of the *initiative* referendum is that it permits individual citizens, having secured a fixed level of support for the measure, to place an item of legislation directly onto the electoral ballot. At first glance it appears to be an instrument of citizen power. However, as Wyn Grant argues in 'Direct Democracy in California: Example or Warning?', the initiative referendum is not a panacea for the ills of democracy and its impact on the practice of democracy is not wholly positive.

As the oldest liberal democratic regime it might be expected that the American model would be one that would have been emulated elsewhere, on the general principle that, if it works, imitate it. However, when attempts have been made to follow the American model, as, for instance in the adoption of presidentialism by many states in South America, the results have not been that successful. Indeed, some political scientists, most notably Juan Linz, have argued that presidentialism is inherently a more unstable form of democratic government than parliamentarism, and that it is only in the rather peculiar circumstances of the United States that it has ever worked.[10] Furthermore, even when the US government has influenced the establishment of institutions in other countries, the result can be quite unlike the American exemplar. For example, 'The United States believed in Germany's "democratic salvation through federalism"', but the kind of

administrative federalism that was to operate in the Federal Republic was
very different from American federalism.[11]

North American Democracy and Political Science

For the political scientist North America should be an important region for
comparative studies of democratization. The three states of continental
North America do share some key features, which would suggest that
comparative analyses might be especially fruitful. For a start, all of them
occupy large territories in comparison with many states in Europe; large
countries pose particular problems of political control – most especially, of
how to link centre with periphery. Furthermore, all of them are countries of
immigration. The indigenous peoples of North America were displaced by
conquerors and settlers from Europe. All three territories were governed by
the European powers, until each obtained independence – and all of them
secured this within a relatively short period: 1783 for the states that formed
the United States in 1787, 1821 for Mexico, and 1867 for Canada. Thus all
three were self-governing before the industrial era.

Nevertheless, North America remains a non-existent region for the
political scientist. Open virtually any world atlas and you will find a section
on North America. Try to find either a book or a university course on the
politics of North America and you will search in vain. There are books and
courses on African politics, on European politics, on South Asian politics
but none, to my knowledge, that focus on North America. For the political
scientist North America has been a region that appears not to have existed.
Of course, its constituent parts do – more books have been written about the
politics of the United States than on the politics of any other country; there
are also a large number of monographs about the Canadian political system
and a smaller number about Mexico. There have even been a few studies
that have compared aspects of the Canadian polity with those of the United
States – including Roger Gibbins' *Regionalism* and Seymour Martin
Lipset's *Continental Divide*, but North America remains conspicuous by its
absence in political science.[12]

It must be admitted that it is unlikely that North America will ever attain
the same status as Europe in political science. In part, this is because the
research agenda for political science is set in the United States, and there is
a marked antipathy among most American political scientists to the idea that
the study of US politics can be, or should be, informed by comparisons with
other countries – irrespective of whether those countries happen to occupy
the same continental land mass as the US itself. In common, for example,
with French political science, American political science is inward-looking
and largely for the same reason – as Stanley Hoffman notes, one of the

features that the political traditions of the two countries have been alleged to share is 'a belief in each country's being an "exception"'.[13]

The point is not that most American political scientists have concluded that their country is an 'exception', for that might well be a valid conclusion, but rather it is a working assumption from the beginning of their careers as researchers that it is an 'exception'.[14] Most political scientists, and there are some notable exceptions, accept some version of the kind of 'mystical exceptionalism' expounded by the political historian Daniel Boorstin to the effect that American history 'can be understood only in terms of working itself out from an original seed which had already determined all subsequent developments in a predefined manner'.[15] From this perspective, not only is there no point in studying American politics from a comparative perspective, but it is actually dangerous to do so since the student may be misled into forgetting just what is 'exceptional' about the United States. In books informed by this perspective other countries are mentioned only in so far as they are useful for emphasizing just what is supposedly different about the United States.

This has produced some faintly ludicrous results. When drafting this essay I selected at random from my bookshelves one of a number of standard textbooks on American politics written in the last 30 years. The one I happened to have chosen provides a good example of the point I am making. Writing in 1970 the author noted: 'The United States of America is unique in many respects, and certainly one of its uniquenesses has to do with the physical setting. In the first place, America is an enormous land mass, far larger, for example, than any single European nation-state'.[16] It never seems to have occurred to him that the neighbouring democracy to the north had a land mass that was even greater than that of the US, and that, if you were going to set the American polity in a broader context, it might be useful to do so by comparing it with a country with which it might seem to have more in common than it would with the European countries. It is important to note that the very best American social scientists have not fallen into this trap, of *assuming* American uniqueness, and it is instructive to compare the quotation above with Seymour Martin Lipset's account of the value of comparing the United States with its northern neighbour.[17]

Changing this 'cult of exceptionalism' is not going to be an easy task. However, the advantages of bringing the United States within the scope of comparative analysis are clear. The next challenge for researchers will be to move beyond the single country studies of the states of North America embraced within this volume, and to examine democratization and democracy in North America on a regional basis. Although such studies are never likely to supplant the single country studies, they will surely be a

significant complement to such studies. In part, this volume is intended to
be a prolegomenon to such work.

NOTES

1. Joel H. Silbey, *The American Political Nation, 1838–93* (Stanford, CA: Stanford University Press, 1991), p.14.
2. See Stanley Elkins and Eric McKitrick, *The Age of Federalism* (Oxford and New York: Oxford University Press, 1993).
3. Dietrich Rueschemeyer, Evelyne Huber Stephens and John D. Stephens, *Capitalist Development and Democracy* (Chicago, IL: University of Chicago Press, 1992), p.134.
4. It has been estimated that at the time of the Revolution between 50 and 75 per cent of free adult males were entitled to vote; Sean Wilentz, 'Property and Power: Suffrage Reform in the United States, 1787–1860', in Donald W. Rogers (ed.), *Voting and the Spirit of American Democracy* (Urbana and Chicago, IL: University of Illinois Press, 1992), p.32. Links between property ownership and the franchise persisted after the Revolution and it was not until the Jacksonian era that virtually all free, white adult males acquired the right to vote.
5. Newfoundland was not part of the settlement and did not become a province of Canada until 1949.
6. See Gordon T. Stewart, *The Origins of Canadian Politics: A Comparative Approach* (Vancouver: University of British Columbia Press), 1986.
7. Reuschemeyer *et al.*, *Capitalist Development and Democracy*, p.199.
8. Will Kymlicka, *Multicultural Citizenship* (Oxford: Clarendon Press, 1995), pp.12–13.
9. See William McGerr, *The Decline of Popular Politics: The American North, 1865–1928* (New York and Oxford: Oxford University Press, 1986), pp.17–21 and Ch.5.
10. Juan J. Linz, 'Presidential or Parliamentary Democracy: Does it Make a Difference?', in Juan J. Linz and Arturo Valenzuela, *The Failure of Presidential Democracy* (Baltimore, MD and London: The John Hopkins University Press), 1994, pp.3–87.
11. J.F.Golay, *The Founding of the Federal Republic of Germany* Second Edition, Chicago, 1965, p.17, cited in William E. Paterson and David Southern, *Governing Germany* (Oxford: Blackwell, 1991), p.145.
12. Roger Gibbins, *Regionalism: Territorial Politics in Canada and the United States* (Toronto: Butterworths, 1982); Seymour Martin Lipset, *Continental Divide: The Values and Institutions of the United States and Canada* New (York and London: Routledge, 1990). Other examples of American-Canadian comparative studies are David M. Olson and C.E.S. Franks, *Representation and Policy Formation in Federal Systems* (Berkeley, CA: Institute of Governmental Studies, University of California, 1993) and Leon D. Epstein, 'A Comparative Study of Canadian Parties', *American Political Science Review*, 58 (1964), pp.46–59.
13. Stanley Hoffman, 'France Self-Destructs', *New York Review of Books*, 28 May 1992, p.25.
14. An important re-examination of arguments about American exceptionalism is Byron Shafer (ed.), *Is America Different? A New Look at American Exceptionalism* (Oxford, Oxford University Press, 1991).
15. Michael Foley's summary of Boorstin's argument in Michael Foley, *Laws, Men and Machines: Modern American Government and the Appeal of Newtonian Mechanics* (London and New York: Routledge, 1990), p.23.
16. William C. Mitchell, *The American Polity* (New York: The Free Press, 1970), p.29.
17. At the beginning of a long article Lipset notes there is much to be gained in 'empirical and analytic terms from a systematic comparative study of Canada and the United States. They have many of the same ecological and demographic conditions, approximately the same level of economic development, and similar rates of upward and downward mobility'. Seymour Martin Lipset, 'Historical Traditions and National Characteristics: A Comparative Analysis of Canada and the United States', *Canadian Journal of Sociology*, 11 (1986), p.114.

Constitutional Angst:
Does American Democracy Work?

NELSON W. POLSBY

The current state of democracy in the United States is estimated against seven characteristics held to define polyarchies: elected officials, inclusive suffrage, the right to run for office, free and fair elections, freedom of expression, alternative information and associational autonomy. The conclusion is that the contemporary United States meets these standards.

I

It is only a small exaggeration to say that among the dubious benefits Americans have received from the collapse of the Soviet Union and its associated authoritarian regimes is an increase in the number and volume of voices saying that democracy in America does not work very well. Evidently an adversarial world order helps to forestall the more corrosive sorts of American self-appraisal. But the current global environment provides no credible military threats to American democracy. This has created what might be called a severe angst-gap in the United States, a gap that anguished voices from all points in the political spectrum are working overtime to fill.

Former members of the cabinet and political advisers to Presidents of the United States, for example, are on record urging fundamental constitutional reform so as to discourage stalemate in decision-making and increase accountability of political leaders to voters.[1] Conservative legislators are sponsoring a variety of constitutional amendments limiting the terms of office of members of Congress, establishing an item veto for Presidents and requiring balanced budgets.[2] A new liberal journal of public affairs says in its manifesto: 'The health of democracy in America, after all, is not good. The relations of politics, money, and the media have deformed our traditions. Cynicism about politics is pervasive; "politician" and "bureaucrat" are terms of abuse. Voter turnout has fallen to a level that ought to be a national embarrassment ... .'[3]

Referring to a 'rigged political system' a liberal public interest lobbyist charges 'the current system of financing elections for the U.S. Congress is patently unfair'. He says, 'we are actually losing our ability to have real congressional elections'.[4]

In the wake of a protracted struggle over the size and shape of the US budget a few years ago, several mainstream news magazines – *Newsweek, US News, Business Week* – declared the American political system bankrupt and called for massive reforms.[5]

One thoughtful observer wrote:

> I remain deeply concerned that the nation is not addressing (a) the way in which our tax system penalizes thrift and rewards consumption, (b) the problems of the underclass, (c) the continuing decline in educational achievement (especially in mathematics, science, and engineering) and in public education generally; and (d) our persistent and destructive underinvestment in our public institutions, including the schools, the bureaucracy, and the courts. I keep thinking that there must be some flaw that prevents us from reaching these issues until they turn into disasters.[6]

There is an ebb and flow to expressions of this sort that suggests they might be responding to passing events or other ephemeral stimuli, but somehow the very volume and diversity of complaints has set observers to wondering if underlying causes of distress are few or many, responsive to amelioration (and hence *problems*) or so deeply 'sown in the nature of man', as James Madison put it, as to constitute *conditions* with which Americans must simply learn to live. Are the opinions of those who contribute to public discussion well informed and diagnostically acute? Are they shaped more toward expressing a short-run political agenda or fulfilling the political ambitions of complainants or will they stand scrutiny on the merits? Are proposed solutions likely to prove effective or are they worse than the disease as described?

When critics ask: why doesn't an institution give us policies that we need, the sovereignty of the need is, in general, unexamined. How, after all, can Americans not pay attention to social injustice, decaying infrastructure, or the spotty coverage of national health insurance? The idea that forces in the American system having political legitimacy – and political clout – might disagree about needs and that American political institutions might reflect these disagreements is liable to be taken merely as a restatement of the problem rather than as an explanation accounting for the phenomenon in question.

Thus the failure of political institutions to deliver some specified policy outcomes may or may not reflect malfunctions. Institutions are not obliged a priori to gratify the policy preferences even of enlightened members of the community, especially if they are, in one legitimate arena or another, outnumbered. What issues a political system addresses at any given time –

the content of the political agenda – is of course a very important question, and in fact not a great deal is known about how differing structures lead to different agendas. It is therefore necessary to distinguish between (1) structural barriers to the consideration of issues and (2) differing prescriptions arising from different views in the population of the proper resolution of issues. Thus a threshold question is whether complaints about the political system are the work of persons who do not like a set of political outcomes and therefore ask for a recount as a tactic in an ongoing political battle. Is it actually true, for example, that the US political system does not *address* problems associated with 'the underclass'? Or that the United States has no tax policies – that is, does not *address* – issues related to thrift and consumption? And so on. Or is it the case that a given critic simply does not happen to like the current set of policy outcomes? I propose to stipulate that sour grapes in the political arena is not what the bulk of contemporary manifestations of constitutional angst are about in order to give due weight to the cumulative impact of the indictment, and the remarkable ideological spread of the dissatisfied population.

Nor is the heart of the matter a lack of policy innovation or political change. It is not the case that the American political system is impervious to political or policy innovation.[7] Despite the laggard performance of the US system on some issues connected to the general welfare, it is possible to point since the New Deal to massive changes in American public policy more or less without reliance upon large-scale institutional reform. A short list of these changes (not all in the same direction) would include:

(1) the civil rights revolution;

(2) the policy changes associated with the 89th Congress (for example, medicare);

(3) the Reagan retrenchment.

Policy changes associated with elections (of 1964, of 1980, and possibly of 1994) or with evolving majorities in the appellate courts responsive to cases and controversies constitute evidence for the proposition that 'the system' as currently organized produces political innovation and that in order to get policy changes – even very drastic changes – it may not be necessary to change 'the system' (that is, the constitutional or institutional framework) at all. This presupposes, to be sure, that the American political system already meets minimal criteria of democratic practice. If a political system can be shown to be undemocratic, this demonstration would lend considerable credence to the arguments of critics who are unhappy with the policies that system may produce. That is to say, such policies could be regarded as illegitimate. Thus it seems important to ask whether the political system in the United States meets elementary criteria generally thought to be essential to democracy.

II

It may be helpful in this connection to draw upon what many scholars will recognize as a classic formula describing 'processes and institutions of large-scale, representative democracy of the type developed in the 20th Century', or , in Robert Dahl's language, a polyarchy, in order to see whether we may consider the United States to be an example.[8] Polyarchies are held to be defined by seven institutional characteristics, which we can use as a baseline for gauging contemporary American governmental performance. These characteristics are:

(1) elected officials;

(2) inclusive suffrage;

(3) the right to run for office;

(4) free and fair elections;

(5) freedom of expression;

(6) alternative information;

(7) associational autonomy.[9]

The first four characteristics have to do with elections, of which the United States has a great many.

Elected Officials

At the national level, virtually all major policy-making in the United States requires action by elected officials and, to a degree unmatched elsewhere, unelected policy-makers not only serve formally at the pleasure of elected officials but typically in practice last in office only as long as the elected officials who appointed them. This is not true of the unelected bureaucratic mandarins who dominate policy-making in most advanced democratic nations. Unlike many democratic nations, the United States also has a full complement of elected officials at an intermediate distance from ordinary citizens, at the state level, with a range of responsibilities that within their sphere (for example, police, road maintenance) more or less correspond to those of national officials, and there is yet another, local, level, with in many cases a rather full array of elected officials at that level too, including, for example, elected school boards and trustees of public sector organizations having specialized functions, such as transportation, water supply, or waste management.

Presumably the main point about having elected officials predominate in the making of public policy is that if the general trend of public policy is unsatisfactory, or if one or more incidents with respect to public policy or other aspects of the conduct of public officials incur the disapproval of the general populace, then at the next election the officials in charge can be replaced. Behaviour consequent to the threat of replacement, and to the desire of officials to forestall replacement, as well as to the actual replacement of public officials from time to time, are all thought to provide the sort of significant links between followers and leaders that entitles a political system to be classed as democratic.

The second criterion identifies more fully the population which elected officials need to take into account in maintaining a democratic leader-follower relationship. Such a relationship requires of the followers that they be permitted in large numbers to vote. Hence:

Inclusive Suffrage

Like many modern democracies, the United States was late in granting suffrage to women (1920). More scandalously, Americans descended from African slaves were, with the acquiescence of the legal systems of the states in the southeastern quadrant of the nation, denied the vote for more than a century after the abolition of slaves.[10] The reorientation of the legal system in the 1960s with respect to the voting rights of these citizens was a fundamental achievement. In addition, the age of voting eligibility for all citizens has since 1971 dropped from 21 to 18. The right to vote in the United States is now quite inclusive.

Voting does, however, rely for practical execution on a fair measure of voluntarism, in that most localities require proof of residence as a prerequisite of voting, and require would-be voters to take the initiative to register to vote. This frequently poses some practical problems for the one-third of Americans who change their home addresses in every two-year interval. Thus the extreme geographic mobility of Americans and the highly localized tradition of control over the mechanics of voting has, among other possible factors, limited the actual turn-out of Americans at the polls. Legal restrictions also deny the right to vote to some ex-felons and all non-citizen aliens, of whom the United States has more than most democratic nations, and those declared mentally incompetent.[11]

Thus, over the last quarter-century, half-century and century, notable advances in the inclusiveness of the right to vote have been achieved by the American political system. In the case of the 18-year-old vote, the change came without notable struggle. In the case of women and African-Americans, there was considerable effort, and resistance. Contemporary Americans look back for the most part with incredulity that this should have been the case, since none of these expansions of the right to vote proved even remotely destabilizing over the medium run to the political system. Indeed it is arguable that only the last expansion of the vote, the one that included African-Americans, even had much of an impact on the relative strength of American political parties. Over the short run, the introduction of sizeable increments of African-Americans into the electorate merely strengthened the politically dominant New Deal coalition. Over a slightly longer run, this change in the character of the electorate no doubt contributed by way of backlash to the rise of the Republican party in the south and hence to the transformation of the south into a political entity somewhat more like the rest of the country. Other elements of demographic change and modernization also were pushing the south in the same direction, and so we must conclude that the influence in isolation of the expansion of the suffrage on political change over the last century has been modest.[12]

The Right to Run for Office

The right to run for most public offices is in general not greatly constrained by legal restrictions, but there are important practical obstacles with respect to the more visible and powerful positions. There is no compact way to describe rules of entry to public office in the United States because there is such diversity both in the pathways and in the offices themselves. Each of the 50 states of the union constitutes a separate legal system and political culture, required only by the US constitution to provide a 'republican form of government'. In some states there are large numbers of elective local offices in each locality; in some there are few. Some states encourage the formation of political parties at the local level to manage nomination processes; in some states local parties are banished from the ballot and aspirants to local office must self-start or affiliate with local civic organizations or interest groups.

Because of the widespread use of primary elections as the vehicle of choice for the making of nominations at all levels, some form of advertising in order to reach voters is frequently required. Advertising means finding and spending money, especially when the potential electorate is very large – as, for example, in Congressional districts (population ca. 600,000) or cities of any size. Thus, the scale of American politics and its reliance on popular voting act in lieu of party organization to ration access to public office.

Most successful candidates for elective office nevertheless first gain the nomination of the Democratic or Republican party. These parties are virtually everywhere located respectively to the left and to the right of whatever the current ideological spectrum is, but the actual content of issues dividing the parties frequently varies greatly from state to state. Thus, what may appear to European observers to be a relatively narrow set of alternative, practical, political options, in fact accommodates quite a lot of variety because of the importance nearly everywhere of local considerations. The localism of American political organization is also reflected in the lack of strict party discipline, except on rare occasions, in national and state, and even local, legislatures.[13]

Additionally, candidates run and are elected to public office without party designation at local levels where party labels are forbidden; and a sizeable, but on the whole electorally unsuccessful, flock of minor parties also run candidates for various public offices, up to and including the presidency. Public funding, which provides a substantial fraction of the finance for major party presidential campaigns, is for practical purposes more or less denied smaller parties, but small party candidates for all offices are not required to forfeit an electoral deposit if they do badly at the polls.

Many thoughtful people believe that Americans are living in an era of weak political parties, and that the strengthening of political parties ought therefore to be high on the agenda for public discussion. In some respects, these thoughtful people have a point. But it is probably worth mentioning that the weakness of American political parties has been enormously exaggerated because of the tendency of political observers to focus on the presidential nominating process, where state parties are indeed weak and uninfluential and the news media and primary electorates dominant. A look at the larger picture tells a somewhat different story.

The term political party stands for at least three somewhat different processes. In the first place, it refers to those organizations that nominate candidates for public office, get out the vote, sponsor campaigns, and register new voters. Such organizations tend to have employees (more in election years, fewer in off years), volunteers, offices, and telephones. They are regulated by state laws, and tend to vary quite a lot from state to state, and locality to locality. One thinks of the squeaky-clean politics of the states of the upper Midwest in comparison, let us say, with Louisiana, where former Governor Earl Long once said that when he died he hoped he would be buried in Plaquemines Parish so that he could remain active in politics. Parties as nominating organizations tend to draw their strength from the grass roots, where most of the political business of America is done, and most of the public offices – for state assembly, city council, and so forth – are located.

Political parties are also symbolic entities, constructs that voters carry around in their heads that help structure public opinion and voting behaviour. Most voting Americans consider themselves either Democrats or Republicans – and, indeed, as I mentioned, the vast majority of American public officials are either Democratic or Republican. In recent years, some surveys have detected what has looked like a 'dealignment' of American voters in which unprecedented members of respondents have identified themselves not as Democrats or Republicans but as Independent voters. This trend has appeared to give comfort (or discomfort) to observers who believe that political parties are weakening in their power to command the allegiance of the electorate.

A strong counter-argument points out that what the data really show is that roughly two-thirds of survey respondents who call themselves 'Independent' voters are actually loyal party voters – some Democrats, some Republicans.[14] They may call themselves Independents for many reasons. Americans do not like to be taken for granted, and many individuals evidently enjoy thinking of themselves as free to choose in each election. Indeed they are, but two-thirds of them regularly freely choose, according to what V.O. Key once described as a 'standing decision,' to back one party or the other in the absence of overwhelming incentives to change. What these 'Independent' survey respondents are doing is suppressing their report of this standing decision until the follow-up question about which way they habitually 'lean'. A reasonable conclusion from this way of looking at the evidence is that party loyalty still exerts a strong pull on the opinions and allegiances of most voters and most citizens. There is not very much to be gained by thinking of strategies for strengthening parties in the electorate.

A third aspect of political parties is visible in legislative bodies: city councils, state assemblies and Congress, where for purposes of organizing committees and staffing the body members caucus according to the party banner under which they were elected. At local levels and in one or two states, nonpartisan elections were established by law, mostly during the Progressive era (1890–1920), expressly to inhibit the influence of political parties on legislative activity. This effort has met with only modest success: voters and members generally know who the Democrats are in the formally nonpartisan San Francisco City Council and who the Republicans are in the nonpartisan unicameral legislature of Nebraska.

I do not know of a comprehensive survey that measures the actual extent to which parties currently organize politics and structure the organization and voting of the myriad legislative bodies with which American states and localities are blessed. An effort in that direction by David Mayhew as of 1960 concluded that there were wide variations in the presence of party from place to place.[15] These variations, rooted in the history, economics and demographic profiles of different geographic places, are as good an illustration as I know of the diversity of American political cultures. That such diverse micro-systems fly only two flags, Democratic and Republican, suggests something of the power of the national government. If the activities of the national government were less important, there would be fewer incentives for Texas Democrats to unite with Vermont Democrats and New Jersey Democrats in search of a governing coalition in Congress.

As to Congress, the record-keeping is excellent, and the story of party cohesion there is unequivocal. Owing principally to the emergence of the Republican party in the southern states, the capacity of party caucuses in Congress to structure policy alternatives and achieve party-line voting has never been higher in nearly a century. Parties in Congress are stronger today than at any time in living memory, now that the power of the Dixiecrats to split the Democratic caucus has greatly diminished.

National party organizations today are raising and disbursing sizeable amounts of money, recruiting candidates, coordinating Congressional votes, and structuring the political preferences of millions of American voters. Does this mean that there is nothing to the common perception that American parties are in decline? In one arena, that of presidential nominating politics, parties are in decline. This of course does not constitute an argument that they should be strengthened. Some observers believe that a presidential nominating process such as now exists, featuring self-starting candidates who must compete with other self-starters for the favour of successive primary electorates, the whole show mediated by news organizations, is in some sense more democratic than any process in which political parties take a larger role.

The ground for this belief has always seemed to me shaky, resting as it does exclusively on the observation that more people 'participate' in primary elections than in the alternative delegate-selecting schemes – principally caucuses of party faithful – that prevailed in many states before they were outlawed by the Democrats in the party reforms of 1969–70. The more 'participants', the argument went, the more 'democracy'.

A more fine-grained analysis might have asked two further questions: (1) what was it that participants were able actually to do? and (2) did this participation embed itself in the overall process so that primary electorates could be said to be more representative of the overall party electorate or national electorate, and better able, therefore, to express the preferences of the great mass of voters than the smaller number of participants they supplanted?

As virtually everyone now agrees, it was on these latter two points that the new arrangements fell down and proved to be a severe disappointment. State party elites merely gave way to those elites best able to manipulate the primary process. Presidential elections became strangely anomalous in the American political system in which the majority party, the Democrats, winners of most elections to state assemblies, governorships, House and

Senate, lost the Presidency time and again.

Why? The most persuasive argument in explaining this anomaly is that the reforms compelled a presidential nominating process in which coalition-building among party leaders was discouraged and factional mobilization – each candidate trying to survive each primary election by bringing his and only his voters to the polls – became the strategy of choice. In the end game, therefore, that party with the most factions, and the most disagreements, the Democrats, had the hardest job of putting the pieces together to fight a general election. Thus, strengthening the parties in the Presidential nominating process really means strengthening state parties at the expense of candidates. It means making the Democrats more competitive in general elections. It means restoring coalition building as a prime goal for candidates.[16]

What caused state parties to exit the process was overregulation by the national Democratic party. State party leaders were told that delegates would not be seated at the national convention unless the delegate selection process in the states, and its outcomes, met a long laundry list of conditions. This restricted the options of party leaders and caused them not only to resort to primary elections but also to insulate most other party business from the presidential race, so as to protect against an unpredictable influx of single-shot enthusiasts.

If regulation was the proximate cause of the exit of state parties from the delegate selection process, presumably deregulation would help in restoring their participation. Two notes of caution need to be sounded in this connection. First, it is naive to think that all state parties are as they were 20 years ago. So the best it is reasonable to hope for is that the restoration of incentives for state parties to control their presidential nomination delegations will increase the ties between presidential selection and other party organizational activities – candidate recruitment, voter mobilization and so on. Some state party elites will prove to be so unrepresentative and hide-bound as to be unable to help in building a winning Presidential coalition. But others will come back into the system, and constitute a force for party cohesion. Results, in short, will vary.

Second, there may be a very few regulations that the national parties will find it prudent to retain. Prohibition against racial exclusion in the delegate selection process is an obvious example. Perhaps, for historically sufficient reasons, it is the only such example.

Free and Fair Elections

With the advent of voting machines and the decline of strong, monopolistic local parties, corruption in the counting of votes and in the general administration of elections has in recent decades become a rarity. Thus, with respect to the four criteria of polyarchy pertaining to elections, American political institutions appear, with the indicated reservations, comfortably to qualify. Indeed, over the last few decades on most dimensions the United States has made modest gains, and in the case of the suffrage of African Americans, dramatic gains.[17]

The three remaining criteria of polyarchy refer to freedoms of information, of expression and of association, all explicitly guaranteed by the first and fourteenth amendments to the US constitution and consequently secured by judicial review and by the prevalence in the United States of a culture of adversary legalism. This culture facilitates recourse to the courts as a means of vindicating the constitutional rights of individuals and of institutions specialized to the expression of political views.

Alternative Information

In general, the legal climate governing journalistic practice in the United States – weak libel laws, strong First Amendment to the Constitution – encourages the printing or the broadcast of nearly any information that may be in a journalist's possession. Thus it is arguable that an unusually wide range of information characteristically becomes available to citizens about the leaders and the policies upon whom they must pass judgment. This conclusion is hotly disputed by observers who are inclined to the belief that a sort of Gresham's law of information operates in which trivia drive out information more relevant to the disposition of public policy.[18] In general, however, the pessimistic view of informational constraints on voter choice is more likely to focus on overload or irrelevancy than successful concealment.

As recently as the presidency of John Kennedy, manipulation by concealment would have been the more pressing problem. Not everyone applauds the evident decline since then in respect for the privacy of public officials. The swift march in norms of journalistic disclosure over the last 30 years along with ever-tightening rules of conduct for officials now regularly take a fearsome toll on the reputations of the more visible public officials.

Because so many decisions are placed in the hands of electorates, in long ballots not only filled with choices for lesser public officials but also, in many states, with initiatives and referendums, the informational needs of voters, even when they do not outrun supply, simply exhaust their patience and their willingness to pay attention. This condition, when it occurs, produces a serious pathology of direct democracy, namely public policy-making defacto not by multitudes of informed voters but by highly manipulative elites who may control the wording – frequently confusing – of measures proffered to the electorate and may undertake effective, but untruthful, advertising campaigns. Presumably a palliative for these pathologies of direct democracy is representative democracy, because representatives can devote time and intelligence and staff and specialized knowledge to deliberation on measures that come before them, including those measures that would strain the cognitive capacities of more casual participants.

The cognitive and informational problems of direct democracy do plague American electorates from time to time, especially in a progressive large state like California where referendums are an entrenched method of policy-making. Similar problems afflict proposals to limit the terms of legislators by initiative, an extremely popular measure everywhere and successfully enacted in those states – roughly half of them – where initiatives are permitted by the state constitution. Such proposals seek to cripple the cognitive capabilities of legislatures by limiting the experience they can accumulate, thus creating new informational problems for democratic policy making.[19]

So while political information is in many respects a free good, with television sets in over 90 per cent of homes, several cable channels devoted to nothing but news, highly professionalized news coverage on the main networks, and daily newspapers also widely and cheaply available, given what a citizen needs to know to make all the decisions that citizens must make, it still may not be enough.

There is no doubt, however, that there is a lot of information out there and that there are alternative sources. Journalistic practices rather than centralized political regulation frequently lead to convergence of coverage and create central tendencies in the content of the news media. These central tendencies as often as not are hostile to incumbents of office, an infrequently examined bias of the news media but not something that reduces the desire of incumbents to remain accountable to electorates.

Freedom of Expression

Freedom of expression on the whole operates over a broader band today than was true a few decades ago, as illustrated, for example, in the wide, public availability of printed words that once would have been seized by the postal service or shut down by local vice squads. Sexual minorities now freely exercise their rights to express themselves. In the political sphere voices of dissent are regularly heard, and in some cases widely publicized. Some of these voices are extremely divisive, and some perform acts, for example, flag burning, public marching and picketing, that stretch the meaning of speech.[20] Mostly, these acts have received legal protection under the First Amendment freedom of speech rubric.

Associational Autonomy

Opportunities to associate unconstrained by the government seem to the naked eye to be as rich and varied today as when Toqueville remarked on the profusion of voluntary associations in the America of a century and a half ago. I know of no census of such organizations but can observe that with respect to at least one subset there has been a notable recent increase. This is the subset making headquarters in Washington for the purpose of influencing the national government. The news media attempt to keep track of such organizations and their number seems to be growing.[21] This suggests that the capacity of citizens, variously organized, to express their views to the government is at least being maintained.

Interest groups have more than one purpose. A function collateral to that of attempting to influence the government is the building of the sort of social capital that helps hold society together. Recently an interesting argument has been made that those sorts of voluntary organizations that nurture political skills and civic trust have suffered a notable decline in the United States over the last few decades.[22] It is not an argument that has as yet been fully tested empirically. At least a few elements must still be sorted out: the extent to which the decline in voluntary organizational life mirrors the entry of women into the paid work force, for example, might lead analysts to think of the time of citizens as having been traded off rather than wasted. Electronic and other sophisticated forms of communication responsive to voluntary manipulation may have liberated Americans from the geographic constraints of primary group interaction and therefore redistributed rather than obliterated associational life. There is a regular progression in the preferences of Americans that replaces batch processing of all sorts – trains, trolleys, apartments, bowling leagues – with customized, independently controlled lives – cars, suburbs, bowling alone, or in small groups. My own belief is that even after these aspects of the argument are fully worked through, substantial justifications for concern about the long-run health of the primary group foundations of the modern American policy will remain.[23]

The matter is, I believe, extremely complex. The loosening of tribal primary group bonds, for example, may be a necessary condition for the growth of personal freedom, and especially the extension of freedom to disadvantaged minorities.[24] Analysts of American democracy are on the verge of a valuable and invigorating debate.

I think nevertheless it is possible to conclude that by reasonably objective standards contemporary American democracy meets criteria classifying it as a vigorously functioning polyarchy, and that trends over the last 30 years or so, on most relevant dimensions, have shown improvement.

III

Harold Wilensky has proposed a sensible set of criteria for assessing the adequacy of contemporary policy outcomes.[25] He has suggested that a given array of political outcomes might be regarded as unsatisfactory or at least problematic if (1) many or all other nations similarly situated displayed a different pattern of outcomes, (2) at least some US political elites wanted to move toward the international norm, (3) public opinion generally supported the indicated move. Examples would be gun control and national health insurance. They point to the strong possibility that there are organizational anomalies in the ways the United States deals with at least some sorts of regulatory issues and issues of public expenditure as compared with the rich parliamentary democracies of Western Europe.

In fact, we all know perfectly well that the US political system incorporates many features that from the standpoint of most western democracies constitute organizational anomalies. Foremost among these is a separation of powers the chief distinctive feature of which is not a strong president but a strong Congress. It is a common mistake in the conventional taxonomies of democratic political systems to classify the United States as an idiosyncratically successful presidential regime in amongst a rather ramshackle set of presidential systems to be contrasted with broadly successful parliamentary regimes.[26]

But the point that needs to be grasped about the American political system is not that so much authoritative policy-making resides in the hands of a President but rather that so much power is held in tension and shared between President and Congress – a separated system, as Charles O. Jones rightly calls it, entailing multiple points of initiative and of veto.[27] An important consequence for the making of policy is that a separated system strikes a completely different balance than parliamentary regimes between what my colleagues Bruce Cain and Nathaniel Persily call the tyranny of the majority versus the tyranny of the status quo.[28] Significant movement in public policy in a status quo-friendly system like the US separated system frequently requires a far more concentrated dose of political will, skill and luck than in the smaller western European democracies – and they are all much smaller than the United States. But when the movement takes place, it is more likely to enjoy wide legitimacy and is less likely to be reversed.

I will not dwell on the pathologies of parliamentary regimes: insufficiently legitimate, seesaw policy-making for the majoritarian systems following the Westminster model; stasis, cycling, the tyranny of small minorities, and over-reliance upon bureaucrats for the non-majoritarian, proportional representation variant. In the United States, bureaucrats do not have the power to break stalemates between Congress and President. Rather bargains leading to supermajorities must be sought by elected officials. Policy proposals can be successfully resisted between elections, and elections settle less about the future course of policy-making than is true in the parliamentary democracies.

The US organizational design is not to be recommended to all nations seeking a constitution. But it is reasonably well adapted to the tasks of dealing with the myriad concerns of a sizeable, extended republic, whose far-flung constituent parts may rightly worry about excessive governmental activity at the centre adverse to their immediate interests. Thus the size and heterogeneity, by section, occupation, generation, ethnicity, religion and language, of the US population may readily account at a minimum for the existence of interests strongly supporting multiple points of veto in a constitutional design. This design, at any rate, is what the United States has.

There are added constitutional complications, notably federalism, which favours the decentralized application of policy, and the adversarial legalism that proceeds from the empowerment of judicial review inherent in a written Bill of Rights. These varied elements of constitutional design, which sustain the underlying heterogeneity of interests in a large and diverse American population, seem to me adequate to explain patterns of policy outcomes differing from outcomes in smaller, more tightly organized parliamentary democracies.

Despite the drastic differences between the scale of the American polity and that of the polities with which it is compared, it must also be said that it is not at all uncommon for policy innovation in the United States to build on examples furnished by the smaller parliamentary democracies.[29] Evidently observers do not find it remarkable that this should be the case; but they should. The size and demographic variety of a nation's population deeply affects its governability and especially by democratic means. Instead of marvelling that the United States is not more like Norway (population 3.5 million Norwegians) or the United Kingdom (one-fourth the population of the United States, where the Welsh, Scots and Irish are the predominant sources of demographic and tribal diversity) observers might better focus on the remarkable fact that the United States maintains civil peace and expands civil rights even as well as it does.

In this the United States is more akin to the Low Countries, with their deep and institutionalized divisions of language and religion.[30] Characteristic American solutions to problems of civil peace in the face of diversity have differed from those of Belgium and the Netherlands, however. They exploit the size of the nation via such devices as geographic mobility, economic expansion, and cross-cutting cleavages.

If we accept the premise that tribalism is a human universal, then the incarceration of Japanese Americans in World War II, the exclusion of Jews from universities and the professions in the 1920s and 1930s, the ruthless persecution of Mormons, the removal of Indian tribes, and the maintenance of a brutal racial caste system in the pre-1960 south seem less remarkable than the eventual alleviation, reversal or abandonment of all these social policies by the American political system. Looking, moreover, at the overall record of Western Europe during a comparable time period it is not at all clear that despite its organizational singularities the American approach to democratic self-government suffers greatly by comparison.

NOTES

1. Lloyd N. Cutler and C. Douglas Dillon, 'Can We Improve on Our Constitutional System?', *Wall Street Journal* (15 Feb. 1983); and Cutler, 'To Form a Government', *Foreign Affairs* 59 (Fall 1980), pp.126–43.
2. *The Contract With America* (available from the House Republican Conference) and Kenneth J. Cooper and Helen Dewar, '100 Days Down But Senate To Go For Most "Contract" Items', *Washington Post*, 9 April 1995, p.A6.
3. Paul Starr, 'Of Out Time', *The American Prospect* 1 (Spring 1990), p.9.
4. Fred Wertheimer, testimony before the Task Force on Campaign Finance Reform, Committee on House Administration, U.S. House of Representatives, 28 May 1991.
5. Weeks of 6 April 1992, and 13 April 1992.
6. Private communication.
7. Nelson W. Polsby, *Political Innovation in America* (New Haven, CT: Yale University Press, 1984).
8. Robert A. Dahl, 'Polyarchy' (1995), a manuscript prepared for the *Encyclopedia Italiana.*
9. These seven characteristics or criteria seem to me roughly comparable to and possibly a bit more user-friendly than Dahl's earlier, more technical, statement in *A Preface to Democratic Theory* (Chicago, IL: University of Chicago Press, 1956), p.84.
10. In general, see Gunnar Myrdal, *An American Dilemma* (New York: Harper & Row, 1969 (1944)).
11. See Raymond E. Wolfinger and Steven J. Rosenstone, *Who Votes?* (New Haven, CT: Yale University Press, 1980).
12. See Earl Black and Merle Black, *Politics and Society in the South* (Cambridge, MA: Harvard University Press, 1987).
13. David B. Truman, 'Federalism and the Party System', in Arthur W. MacMahon (ed.), *Federalism, Mature and Emergent* (New York: Columbia University Press, 1955), pp.115––36.
14. Bruce E. Keith, David B. Magleby, Candice J. Nelson, Elizabeth Orr, Mark C. Westlye and Raymond E. Wolfinger, *The Myth of the Independent Voter* (Berkeley, CA: University of California Press, 1992).
15. David R. Mayhew, *Placing Parties in American Politics* (Princeton, NJ: Princeton University Press, 1986).
16. See Nelson W. Polsby, *Consequences of Party Reform* (New York: Oxford University Press, 1983).
17. After controlling for education and income, African American voters now vote roughly at the same rate as white Americans. See Raymond E. Wolfinger, 'Improving Voter Participation', forthcoming in Paul E. Frank and William G. Mayer (eds.), *What To Do: Recommendations for Improving the Electoral Process* (Boston, MA: Northeastern University Press, 1994).
18. See, for example, Cass Sunstein, *Democracy and the Problem of Free Speech* (New York: The Free Press, 1993).
19. Nelson W. Polsby, 'Constitutional Mischief', *The American Prospect* (Summer 1991), pp.40–43.
20. For example, see Donald Downs, *Nazis in Skokie: Freedom, Community and the First Amendment* (Notre Dame, IN: University of Notre Dame Press, 1985).
21. Jeffrey Berry, *The Interest Group Society*, 2nd edition (Glenview, IL: Scott, Foresman, 1989).
22. Robert D. Putnam, 'Bowling Alone', *Journal of Democracy* 6 (Jan. 1995), p.65.

23. As I suggest in *Consequences of Party Reform*, especially pp.131ff.
24. For an exceptionally fair-minded treatment of the trade-offs, see Alan Ehrenhalt, *The Lost City* (New York: Basic Books, 1995).
25. In a paper at an Institute of Governmental Studies conference in Berkeley, 'What's Wrong with the American Political System?', 5–7 July 1991.
26. Juan Linz, *The Failure of Presidential Democracy* (Baltimore, MD: Johns Hopkins University Press, 1994); Fred Riggs, 'The Survival of Presidentialism in America: Para-Constitutional Practices', *International Political Science Review*, Vol.9, No.4 (1988), pp.247–78.
27. Charles O. Jones, *The Presidency in a Separated System* (Washington, DC: Brookings Institution, 1994).
28. Bruce E. Cain and Nathaniel Persily, 'Legislative Accountability: Could California's Legislature Be More Accountable Under a Parliamentary Form of Government?', paper presented at the California Constitutional Reform conference, Institute of Governmental Studies, University of California at Berkeley, 8–10 June 1995.
29. Polsby, *Political Innovation in America* (New Haven, CT: Yale University Press, 1984).
30. Arend Lijphart, *The Politics of Accommodation*, 2nd edn. (Berkeley: University of California Press, 1975); Lijphart, *Democracy in Plural Societies* (New Haven, CT: Yale University Press, 1977).

The Poverty of Canadian Politics?

GORDON T. STEWART

Political leadership is a key variable in the contemporary process of democratization. Powerful political leaders were also a salient feature of Canada's transition from the authoritarian, governor-controlled regimes in the early nineteenth century to modern democratic conditions in the twentieth century. Canada's political leadership tradition, which valued compromise and accommodation, is often hailed as exemplary but has come in for considerable criticism since 1982 as Canadian politicians continue to fail in their attempts to find a basic constitutional definition of the Canadian state acceptable to Quebec and the rest of Canada. This article assesses the Canadian tradition and argues that the image of past Canadian leaders has conventionally been idealized. An important lesson to be learned from the Canadian case is that leaders who assisted in the transition to democracy in North America worked in generally favourable conditions of economic and territorial expansion and often resorted to party building techniques of patronage, influence and corruption which are denounced when used by contemporary leaders in new democratic polities.

Is Canada a useful case study which might throw light on political democratization in the late twentieth century? The answer to that question is more problematic now than the one which would have been given only a short time ago. Canadian political culture enjoyed a favourable press in the post–1945 era until the failures at constitutional change between 1982 and 1992, and the potential disintegration of the Canadian state, tarnished the image of Canadian political leaders. Moreover, Canada's transition to democracy began in the early decades of the nineteenth century when conditions were far removed from those currently obtaining in states attempting to coax a democratic culture into existence. The old view of Canada's transition to democracy was that Canadian politicians had done a remarkable job in navigating the transition from authoritarian colonial regimes of the 1790–1830 era to the democratic polity of the mid- and late-nineteenth century. The perennial tensions between English and French Canadians, the regional pulls from the West and the Maritimes and the challenge presented by the American leviathan to the south all contributed, it was argued, to a peculiarly effective kind of Canadian politics.

Politicians, to be successful, had to become skilled in compromise and accommodation to make Canada hang together domestically. As they negotiated a Canadian international identity in the interstices between the United States and British empires, the politicians also developed precocious

skills in the international arena. Canadian politicians, public servants and
diplomats in the post-Second World War era therefore viewed their political
traditions as having created an exemplary political culture in which
politicians and parties not only became skilled in the art of compromise but
had their entire centre of gravity in the politics of mutual accommodation.
It may have made Canadian politics and politicians dull to outsiders, but it
kept the country together and allowed Canada to play a constructive role in
the United Nations and other international arenas.

This rosy view of Canadian politics has recently come under challenge.
The failure of the 1992 referendum and the resurgence of regional
resentments in the West has called into question the skills of the Canadian
political classes. To determine if Canada holds any useful lessons for other
countries going through democratization it is necessary to examine this
more pessimistic view of the old Canadian success story and assess what is
left. In the analysis that follows, while commentary will be made on some
general features of the evolution of political culture in Canada, the main
focus will be on the performance of political leadership.

This line of analysis may be justified on the grounds that Canadian
political culture since 1867 has been characterized, among other things, by
a series of strong Prime Ministers from John A. Macdonald (1867–74,
1878–91), Wilfrid Laurier (1896–1911), William Lyon Mackenzie King
(1921–30, 1935–48), to Pierre Trudeau (1968–84), each of whom held
office for long periods and each of whom had a palpable impact on the
political culture of the day. Even in a recent Brookings Institution report on
Canada, the role of a Prime Minister features prominently amidst the more
standard statistical and social scientific analysis of trends and issues.

Andrew Stark points out that in order to understand the most influential
response in English Canada to the Quebec question it is essential to
understand the ideology of former Prime Minister Trudeau and the manner
in which his thinking has informed anglophone and federalist Quebecois
views. Stark reminds us of 'the power that ideas held over the man, the
dominance that the man held over his government and the influence of that
government on a generation'.[1] While none of his predecessors took such an
intellectualised approach to politics, all of them had a similar impact on the
political world of their time.

While this approach, focusing on leadership, reflects the peculiarities of
the evolution of Canadian political culture and the distinctive role played by
federal Prime Ministers, it may be deemed more generally pertinent because
in several of the countries attempting the transition to democracy in the late
twentieth century the role of political leaders is clearly a critical one, from
Boris Yeltsin in Russia to Vaclav Havel in the Czech Republic and Nelson
Mandela in South Africa.

The case that the historical record of Canadian political leaders is a dismal one rests on the brute fact that after 150 years or so of democracy the Canadian state seems on the brink of collapse. Since Canadian confederation was established in 1867 numerous attempts to find a constitutional framework acceptable to all Canadians have failed. No other modern, industrialized, urbanized, high per-capita income country has such a long record of futility in such a fundamental aspect of national life.

The 1992 referendum was the most ambitious attempt so far to address this basic feature of Canada. It was comprehensive in nature, addressing not only the ancient vexation of Quebec's place in Canada but other central issues that had been opened up by the ten years of constitutional debate since the patriation of the British North America Act in 1982. The Charlottetown accord, on which the referendum turned, proposed to recognize Quebec as a distinct society thus providing a legal setting within which Quebec could continue its efforts to preserve its language and culture within Canada and anglophone North America; it proposed a wide-ranging recognition of the autonomy of aboriginal peoples; and it tried to encompass reforms of the Senate and the working of Parliament which would allow for more influence and recognition of Canada's regions.

The defeat of the referendum seems to be a confirmatory sign of the ineptness of political leadership. This is especially so since post-referendum polls showed that a common discontent among voters was a sense of distrust in the politicians who had devised the scheme. There were of course a range of other factors at work to explain the failure of the referendum. Inside Quebec, polls found that voters thought Robert Bourassa had made too many concessions, including Quebec's historical weight in the Senate. Outside Quebec the 'no' voters thought Quebec had won too much, including a permanent fixed number of seats in the Commons irrespective of future demographic trends which would likely reduce the percentage of Quebec's population in Canada. Some voters in the West were fearful that the aboriginal clauses would give too much power to Amerindians.

In the end, the only group in Canada which gave unequivocal support were in fact the aboriginal peoples who believed that they had finally secured territorial recognition and legal rights denied to them since the period of conquest, and the absorption and marginalisation of the nineteenth and twentieth centuries. Yet behind this array of explanations for the failure of the referendum there was one common thread – dissatisfaction with the political leaders who devised this ungainly solution. As *Maclean's* remarked in its post-mortem editorial 'the referendum campaign stands as the most sweeping rebuff to elected politicians in the country's 125 years'.[2]

The constitutional debacle can be seen as a consequence of poor democratic skills by the nation's political leaders. Although a belated attempt was made to consult ordinary people across Canada, through a series of public forums, the entire process since 1982 had been driven by decisions made in closed meetings between provincial Premiers and federal Prime Ministers.[3] As an extension of this view that the negotiations were being conducted in a remote, even secretive, manner there was a related perception that participants, most notably Prime Minister Mulroney himself, were using the constitutional occasion to shore up their own political fortunes. Some commentators argued that Mulroney was appeasing Quebec in order to strengthen the Progressive Conservative party's position inside that province. Mulroney's 'approach to policy', charged one of his critics, 'is too partisan and event driven'.[4] This widespread perception that the methods and goals of political leaders were suspect led Canada's Ambassador to the United States, Adam Gottleib, to remark that people in Canada were 'alienated from politicians'.[5]

It is fair to note at this point that political leaders in other democracies have suffered from similar criticisms and that confidence in political leadership from Germany, to France, Italy, Britain and the United States is at low ebb. Indeed, ever since the publication in 1975 of the Trilateral Commission's report entitled *The Crisis of Democracy*, there has been a scholarly literature arguing that all modern democracies are facing such persistent fiscal, social and cultural challenges that there is some reasonable doubt about the ability of democratic states to survive.[6] But the case in Canada seems more serious than Britain and Italy, for example, because the doubts center not on issues of economic policy, corruption, law and order and so on but on the very existence of the state itself. The issue in Canada seems terminal rather than transitory.

The recent inadequate performance of political leaders seems to fit a pattern that has been evident since the creation of Canadian confederation. At no point in modern Canadian history has a Prime Minister been able to articulate a vision of Canada that has appealed to Quebec and Canadians in the different regions. In so far as Prime Ministers have tackled the problem of Canadian diversity they have done so by accommodation and expediency. Indeed, one of the hallmarks of Canadian political culture has been taken to be this genius for compromise. The downside is that this political tradition, as was evident between 1982 and 1992, has been unable to produce a vision that will work.

The culture of compromise has its merits. Inside Canada, the tensions between Quebec and English Canada, and the tensions between regions, have been contained historically by careful allotment of cabinet posts in Ottawa, deployment of federal patronage, revenue transfer agreements and other such arrangements between local, provincial and federal administrations. The process is not unique to Canada and is characteristic of other linguistically

segmented democracies. The Dutch scholar Arend Lijphart developed a
theory about elite accommodation as the foundation for stability in such
polities.[7] The strength, ingenuity and success of this behind-the-scenes
tradition must be recognized but in the wake of the 1992 failure it is worth
asking whether these features of Canadian political culture have run their
course and are no longer as fruitful in outcomes as they once were.

The issues at stake here can be illustrated by looking at the records of
Canada's most successful political leaders and the ways in which those
records have their limitations. To begin with the most renowned of all, John
A. Macdonald, it is clear that he simply hoped that in the long run the
French problem in Canada would go away. While he accepted the absolute
necessity of collaboration with French Canadian leaders to form effective
parties and so run Canadian governments – indeed, his entire career was
built on that successful collaboration – he viewed the duality of Canada as
a passing phenomenon that might last as long as a hundred years but would
eventually yield to the assimilationist forces of the anglophone American
and Atlantic world. Throughout his time in office he worked with
politicians from Quebec (George-Etienne Cartier before Confederation and
Hector-Louis Langevin thereafter) to keep French and English in harness at
the national level. Through these leaders French Canadians secured access
to cabinet offices, the federal public service, and a range of other
opportunities and could join with English Canadians in thinking that the
federal system had benefits for them. Macdonald described the French
Canadians as his 'sheet anchor' and he acted on that reality by attending to
their concerns as far as he could without alienating too many voters in
English Canada.

His ingenious balancing-act approach worked. The new nation held
together. In spite of discontent over various issues, Quebec accepted that the
federal state of Canada was on the whole beneficial. But while this success
must be noted it is also worth observing that no constitutional legacy was
left by Macdonald, either in terms of practice or of rhetoric, that has been of
any help in the modern debate. There has always been a question among
historians about what Macdonald had in mind in 1867. At one end of the
spectrum are those who see him simply as a politician trying to get a piece
of legislation through; at the other are those who see Macdonald working
alongside Cartier to create a beginning moment of Canadian federalism in
which French and English Canadians viewed themselves as two founding
peoples. Whatever section of the spectrum one concentrates on, it is difficult
to point to any declaration by Macdonald that might be used today.[8]
Macdonald was not quoted during the 1982–1992 debate as Jefferson might
be in a political debate in the United States, or even Disraeli on the 'two
nations' in a debate about the state of modern British politics.

Macdonald's successors continued this pattern of balancing and compromise in the interests of national unity. Wilfrid Laurier, the first French Canadian Prime Minister, raised the art to an even higher level in the sense that he presented leadership by compromise as a glorious attribute. During the 1896 election campaign he reminded Canadians of Aesop's fable about the struggle of the wind and the sun to determine who was stronger. The more the wind blew and tried to force the man to take off his coat, the tighter the coat was held; but the sun's warmth encouraged the coat to come off. So it was with leadership in Canada – the sunny ways of compromise could achieve much more than attempts to force recognition of rights.

Laurier's great challenge came from the revitalized imperialism which swept across Britain and her settlement colonies in the two decades before the Great War. Most English Canadians wished Canada to play a more active role in the empire; most French Canadians, while remaining loyal to the British colonial state in North America, disapproved of an active role for Canada in imperial expansion. Laurier steered his way through these shoals with great skill. Buffeted by the winds of French Canadian nationalism and English Canadian imperialism, Laurier, even more than Macdonald, raised compromise to the point where it became the hallmark of successful leadership. He could sound somewhat plaintive at times about the lack of understanding accorded to his tacking course but he did articulate a philosophy of compromise which had been instinctual and rhetorically terse in the case of Macdonald.

As he went down to defeat in the 1911 election, Laurier gave eloquent voice to his credo. 'I am branded in Quebec as a traitor to the French', he declared,

> and in Ontario as a traitor to the English. In Quebec I am branded as a Jingo, and in Ontario as a Separatist. In Quebec I am attacked as an Imperialist, and in Ontario as an anti-Imperialist. I am neither. I am a Canadian. Canada has been the inspiration of my life. I have before me as a pillar of fire by night and as a pillar of cloud by day a policy of true Canadianism, of moderation, of conciliation. I have followed it consistently since 1896, and I now appeal with confidence to the whole Canadian people to uphold me in this policy of sound Canadianism which makes for the greatness of our country and of the Empire.[9]

Laurier lost the election which suggests that his attempt to define a Canadianism which transcended current preoccupations with empire in English Canada and with cultural Catholic nationalism in Quebec was not appreciated by contemporaries no matter how much it appealed to later generations of historians. Laurier's paean to compromise became the standard for his successors although they were not quite so verbose in their description of it. This was certainly so for Canada's Prime Minister for most of the 1920s, 1930s and 1940s, William Lyon Mackenzie King. His was more of a cheeseparing approach than Laurier's. As Frank Scott, poet and legal philosopher, co-founder of the Co-operative Commonwealth Federation and political gadfly in Quebec, said of him in a memorable line, 'he did nothing by halves that he could do by quarters'.[10]

Mackenzie King's main achievement was to restructure the relationship with Britain in ways which defused the imperial controversy within Canada. Along with other colonial prime ministers, he worked with the imperial government to redefine empire as commonwealth. Throughout the inter-war years Mackenzie King sought better ties with the United States as a sign that Canada had a new sense of her North American priorities in external relations rather than the old imperial ones. This helped in Quebec where such a North American outlook was taken for granted. As Henri Bourassa observed, French Canadians were 'American by ethnical temperament'.[11] Mackenzie King's methods ensured that when the Second World War broke out Canada made her own declaration of war on Germany in contrast to 1914 when she had entered automatically as a colony of Britain.[12]

In recent times the one prime minister who seems to be an exception to this pattern of keeping peace by accommodation and avoidance of ideology is Pierre Trudeau. His active policy of promoting federal bilingualism across the country and his vision of a Canadian identity, appeared to be an attempt to address the concerns of Quebecois by actual structural and ideological change which dealt with francophones' fundamental complaints. The twin bases of Trudeau's vision were, first, at the level of the state, the idea that federal entities like Canada could embrace more than one cultural or historical nation and that such a multiplicity of sub-nationalisms within the federation could be a source of vitality and strength. Secondly, at the level of the individual, Trudeau envisaged citizens who were cosmopolitan in outlook rather than being rooted exclusively within their native ethnic or national identities.[13]

However, the more Trudeau's day-to-day leadership on this matter is seen in historical perspective, the less it can be viewed is as an exercise in disinterested statesmanship. His emphasis on federal bilingualism did not address the basic issue. The rise of modern nationalism in Quebec meant that federal bilingualism was no longer center stage. For Quebec after the 1960's the key question was how Canada's constitutional system could be altered to allow Quebec to cultivate and defend its francophone culture within the national homeland of Quebec. The question now became one of ensuring that Quebec had the legal power to deploy language legislation that would protect its distinct culture and society.[14]

Quebecois were no longer concerned as they had been in the pre-1914 era of Laurier and Henri Bourassa with francophone minority rights outside of Quebec or with bilingualism throughout federal structures. Trudeau's policies, far from taking this seismic shift into account and trying to incorporate it into a new constitutional arrangement, were designed to destroy modern Quebec nationalism.[15] In much the same way that Mulroney has been criticized for tangling constitutional issues with partisan goals, so Trudeau's approach to the Quebec problem was tainted by his goal of destroying his nationalist critics inside Quebec. It is essential to appreciate that the reaction against Trudeau's view cut across a wide spectrum of opinion in Quebec and was not confined to radical separatist circles. Trudeau's policies were designed to extend Ottawa's powers and to constrain provincial power.[16] This threatened to weaken Quebec's ability to direct its society and culture. Trudeau's entire approach undermined the emergence of a strong province which most Quebecois regarded as essential if they were to retain their francophone identity while remaining part of Canada.

It is telling in this context that Trudeau was responsible for the patriation of the British North America Act in 1982 without securing conditions that would have reassured Quebec that the province would not be subject to the English Canadian majority on basic matters such as language rights, and community rights as distinct from individual rights. Trudeau, in short, was intent while in power on undermining the new Quebec nationalism rather than seeking a constitutional environment within which Canadian and modern Quebec nationalisms could coexist. The entire decade of debate since 1982 was started because of this failure at the outset to get Quebec's acquiescence to the terms of patriation. Because of Trudeau's history on these matters the patriation (with its accompanying Charter of Rights) was viewed in Quebec as a device to thwart Quebec's ability to protect its special culture within Quebec itself. As Christian Dufour put it in his essay *Le defi québecois*, ' ... la société québecoise est depuis 1982 en compétition avec une vision constitutionnalisée du Canada qui ne lui est pas compatible'.[17] Thus even Trudeau's exceptionalism turns out upon closer scrutiny not to be a radical break from to the historical pattern. In spite of his intellectual ingenuity, like all national leaders since 1867, he had failed to put the constitutional debate beyond the level of partisan manoeuvring.

The commonalities in this pattern from Macdonald to Trudeau and Mulroney suggest that there are some deep structures in Canadian political culture. To be sure, each of these leaders was working within particular conditions which led them to chart their own course to preserve political stability and hold the country together but the parallels remain striking. One illuminating line of explanation for these common patterns goes back to the origins of Canadian politics. The political culture of contemporary Canada has been moulded by many economic, social, institutional and international factors that have only made their presence felt in recent decades but there are some orientations that were formed at the point of origin and still make their mark on the Canadian political landscape.

A good example of the kind of phenomenon we are discussing here comes from the field of American politics. During the colonial period before 1776 there was a struggle for power between the British-appointed governors and the local colonial assemblies. Because the governors did not possess the revenue and patronage deployed by the crown's ministers in Britain they were not able to build up sufficient influence to manage the colonial assemblies as the crown's ministers managed Parliament in Britain. For their part, the colonial assemblies watched carefully for opportunities to assert their powers. Thus in contrast to eighteenth-century Britain where executive and legislative activities were intertwined, in the American colonies there were separate executive and legislative spheres. Long before the explicit written imprimatur was placed on this separation during the revolutionary struggle and its attendant constitution-making, American politics had been characterized by a separation of the powers. In short, actual conditions in colonial politics had established a particular orientation which left a permanent mark on the American political landscape.[18]

Looking at the origin period for Canadian politics prior to confederation in 1867, the actual working of politics during the initial transition to democracy left permanent marks on Canadian political culture. Those that concern us here include the tendency of Canadian political leaders to use executive power rather than democratic consultation to address constitutional issues and their penchant for using executive influence and patronage deployment in pursuit of political success. During the struggle for local control of colonial government between 1790 and the 1840s the opposition political leaders mobilized their popular support by promising that once the narrow British-supported ruling groups had been displaced, the Reformers would take over and staff the executive and public service with like-minded individuals. Since the American option of fighting a war for republican independence was a non-starter in Canada, the reform impulse centered on getting opposition supporters from outside the old Tory connections into power.

Once in office the new regimes needed to distribute patronage to their followers throughout the constituencies in order to make sure the old ways had been buried and that local Canadian control had indeed been accomplished. In the course of the transition from governor-dominated regimes to party-based executives, political leaders took over many of the prerogative powers of governors as well as the new power derived from

their electoral strength. These political developments were underway before
the concept of a neutral public service was in place and even before there
was a movement to articulate and defend such a concept.[19] Thus the public
service became the arena in which parties shored up their strength and
extended their reach into society. The forces seemed so natural that
Macdonald could declare openly that 'in the distribution of government
patronage we carry out the true constitutional principle that whenever an
office is vacant it belongs to the party supporting the government'.[20]

Because of the circumstances of their origins the Canadian parties were
not well prepared to deal at the ideological level with identity issues as these
arose in various periods of tension from the 1840s onwards between English
and French Canadians. The preferred method was to defuse the tension by
turning to more cabinet positions for the aggrieved group and prescribing
patronage medicine that would soothe the patient.[21] As the Royal
Commission on Bilingualism and Biculturalism Report observed of the
Laurier regime between 1896 and 1911, 'the distribution of patronage was
the most important single function of the government'.[22] The genius of
Canadian politics was taken to lie in the ability of political leaders to avoid
national debates on identity issues. National leaders were most successful
when they were able to keep at the margins the big, divisive issues between
the two cultures.

The question that naturally arises is why has Canada survived so long if
these disadvantageous features exist within the political culture? The
answer lies at two levels. First, as we have suggested, in spite of the critique
that can be made of Canadian political leaders, they were successful in
terms of their own times. Deployment of patronage in this systematic and
comprehensive manner was a shared value between English and French
Canadians and contributed to the loyalty of both groups within the Canadian
colonial state. Second, for much of the nineteenth century, and arguably
down to the 1960s, Canadians of both language groups shared an important
common assumption that it was important to keep Canada intact to prevent
too much Americanization.

Recent work on the history of national identity has drawn attention to the
importance of the 'other' in providing common ground for such an identity.
Linda Colley in her account of the origins of modern British nationalism has
shown how the disaggregated Scottish, Welsh and English regional
identities were fused into a British one in the heat of the world wide
struggle, including several wars, against France between 1688 and 1815.[23]
In the case of Canada, in contrast to this pattern, most English and French
Canadians had only a fragile basis for a common sense of nationalism.
Many of the historical experiences which forge a national identity have
worked in the opposite direction in Canadian history. Wars, for example,

which have been at the centre of British self-images, have often been unifying forces but Canadians were divided by the war against the Metis in western Canada in 1884–85, the Boer War in South Africa 1899–1902, the Great War 1914–18 and again in the Second World War as the two major ethnic groups disagreed about where Canada's national interest lay in these internal, imperial and European conflicts. There was no common attachment to a flag or to the 1867 British Parliamentary legislation which provided only a serviceable rather than an inspiring 'constitution' which all Canadians could regard with reverence. Canadian history itself was told in two master narratives.

The single most important historical force holding the country together in these divisive circumstances was the view of the United States as the 'other' against which definitions of Canadianism were invented and cherished. English Canadians with memories of the American Revolution and the war of 1812 as influenced by loyalist mythology, and French Canadians fearing absorption into a secular levelling republic, both saw the colonial state of Canada as an entity worth preserving. As Jacques Monet pointed out in his study of Quebec in the 1840s, Quebec at that time, in spite of the battles over language, was ready to defend the British colonial state of Canada to the last cannon shot.[24]

While this fear of the United States lessened by the early decades of the twentieth century, it remained the case that the more conservative political culture in Canada, in both its anglophone and francophone variations, saw benefits in marking out a different course in North America from that of the United States. It is not just coincidence that the powerful surge of separatism in modern Quebec has been accompanied by an opening up of Quebec to the United States. The Free Trade Agreement leads Quebec nationalists to think that the economic ties with the United States can survive separatism and that the local francophone culture will preserve Quebec from the cultural assimilation which so many English Canadian nationalists fear.

It was because of these factors creating loyalty to the colonial state both by English Canadians and French Canadians that Canadian political leaders were successful in holding the country together.[25] They worked within the lowest common denominator political culture assumptions of their day, they addressed issues by a range of compromise techniques, and they held a common view that the struggle to keep Canada separate from American influence and control was a worthwhile national goal. French and English Canadians shared these things in spite of tensions and periodic crises over language issues, the West, the empire and federal–provincial relations.

Identification of these forces at work in Canadian history enables us to appreciate the type of political leadership that became characteristic in

Canada. Once that understanding is in place then the condemnation of Canadian leaders as failures can be put in a fairer perspective. However, to explain and to understand still leaves the indictment that these political traditions that have held the country together for so many years have a downside to them which makes political leaders curiously ineffective when it comes to devising contemporary solutions that would inspire Canadians to think afresh about the future of their country. It has also been pointed out that the traditions of elite accommodation and compromise have ill-prepared Canadian political leaders for dealing with modern interest group politics.[26] The disintegration of the federal Conservative party in the last election is perhaps another hint that these kind of parties with these kind of leaders have reached the end of their usefulness.

The new environment has developed over many years but the main features have become most apparent since the 1960s. The secularized Quebec nationalism which emerged in that decade no longer saw the need to keep up a united Canada in face of perceived threats of Americanization. Above all, most Quebecois saw the urgent necessity for exceptional power at the provincial level to protect and promote the French language inside Quebec. They insisted on recognition of the concept later summed up at Meech Lake in the phrase 'distinct society' so that they would have a constitutional basis upon which to justify language legislation. Moreover, as Canada (including Quebec) found in the post-1945 era that its economy was coming to be more and more bound with that of the United States, the old argument that the Canadian east–west economy (begun with Macdonald's national policy in 1878) was the best option for economic growth made increasingly little sense.

Attempts in the 1960s, 1970s and 1980s to increase trade with Japan and the European Union did not alter the fundamental dependence of the Canadian on the American economy. The signing of the Free Trade Agreement with the United States in 1988 was the culminating moment here. With prospective access to a freer North American market (subsequently enlarged by the North American Free Trade Agreement which included Mexico) there was less need for the traditional federal political structure of Canada within which provinces and regions could pursue economic growth. Thus, in the new context of international economic forces and of the modern nationalism shared by most Quebecois, the historical pattern of Canadian political leadership seemed to have become irrelevant. Conditions had changed to the point where the traditional qualities of behind-the-scenes mediation, elite accommodation, deployment of patronage, no longer worked. Even worse, such features of the system were now viewed (as was revealed by the *Maclean's* post-referendum poll) as harmful.

The lessons to be drawn from this Canadian historical experience are not encouraging for political leaders in emerging democracies. A cardinal point here is that Canadian leaders who assisted in the transition to democracy in North America were working in much more favourable conditions than their counterparts in the contemporary world. At the macro level Canadian leaders had the advantage of being able to rise on the general tide of nineteenth century material progress. While there were recessions in the 1830s and 1870s and lengthy periods of economic sluggishness (compared to the United States), the Canadian colonial state functioned in a general world setting of economic expansion, especially in the two areas that most impinged upon Canada, the British imperial sphere and the continental American one.

Beyond this rising economic tide, there was also a general faith in progress – that societies and economies would improve over time and that poorer groups or states, if they were patient and played by the conventions, would eventually get their place in the sun. Faith in progress is no longer so pervasive in the late twentieth century as it was in the nineteenth. As a recent editorial in *The Guardian Weekly* remarked, assuming it was a piece of common wisdom, 'the world community has long since lost confidence in being able to progress onwards and upwards: now we are only too aware of our shaky ability to preserve the environment and eliminate hunger and poverty'.[27] This new psychological world makes the task of political leaders more difficult as poorer, excluded, marginalized, and resentful social and ethnic groups demand immediate solutions rather than accept deferred promises that general progress will lead to an eventual improvement in conditions for everyone.

A second observation is that there was much more tolerance of practices that would now be considered illegal or at least improper. Canadian political leaders between the 1840s and the modern industrial era used patronage and jobbery in a systematic manner in order to achieve political stability. Such use of power had been legitimized by the nature and timing of Canada's transition from governor-controlled regimes to politician controlled regimes between the 1790s and 1840s. There are still remnants of this culture in contemporary Canada. The appointment of Prime Minister Jean Chretien's nephew to the plum job as Canadian Ambassador to the United States is one such example. Raymond Chretien is undoubtedly superbly qualified but it is unlikely such a choice would have been risked in other western democracies in the 1990s. Several other projects and appointments have led to criticism that the Liberal government is 'still playing the old patronage game'.[28] This tolerance of patronage was in many ways reminiscent of the ways in which political stability was achieved in Britain in the aftermath of the 1688 revolution.

Following the turmoil of the seventeenth-century revolutions, the

English polity became prosperous and stable in the eighteenth century as political leaders in Parliament created voting coalitions and then parties by (among other things) use of patronage and the partisan distribution of government business.[29] The use of such techniques in Canada was made easier because the territorial expansion in the West and administrative expansion in the old provinces throughout the period between the 1840s and 1950s gave political leaders at all levels ample opportunities for distributing rewards. Such an expansive landscape in the public service enabled politicians to build their parties and achieve political stability. The parties were able to develop a pervasive reach in society, with active local organizations spurred by hopes of local notables receiving rewards. Ritualistic events in public settings such as the great party picnics in the summer months were additional signs of the cultural importance of parties in nineteenth-century Canada.[30] The ability of the parties to be so culturally and socially significant and deliver rewards, and hope of rewards, in this manner were some of the bases for successful democracy in Canada.

Many of these methods would be frowned upon in the late twentieth century, certainly by the international community, and would lead to charges of corruption and narrow partyism. Canadian politicians would join Britain's John Major, France's Edouard Balladur, Spain's Felipe Gonzalez and Italy's Silvio Berlusconi in newspaper articles about the 'sleaze factor'.[31] John A. Macdonald's drinking binges would be compared to those of Boris Yeltsin. The case of even such an iconic figure as Nelson Mandela in South Africa being subject to criticism about patronage is a telling sign of this environment. In addition to the higher standards now expected of political leaders, none of the transitional states has the luxury of territorial and administrative expansion within which Canadian leaders could operate almost with abandon. Thus contemporary leaders have the burden of higher, more 'modern' standards of public behaviour and are working in more restricted settings for party building.

A third aspect of conditions during the transition to democracy which made things easier for Canadian leaders was the benefit which Canada derived from proximity to the United States. This is perhaps a provocative case to make because so much of the history of Canada's relations with the United States were characterized by wars, war scares, cross-border tensions and sustained mutual suspicion and incomprehension. But if the trade and economic relations are followed as distinct from the political, cultural and even diplomatic aspects, the story is one of steady integration of the North American economy culminating the Free Trade Agreement of 1988.

All Canadian governments from the 1840s onward – that is, from the moment they were able to set their own economic agenda separate from the British imperial one – worked to achieve closer trade links with United

States. Although this goal was thwarted during the protectionist era in the United States from the 1870s to the 1930s, trade increased simply because of proximity and 'natural' patterns of commerce. As Arthur Meighen, Conservative Prime Minister in the 1920s, observed in this context, if he had 'control of the tariff policy of the United States for a period of ten years [he could] do more for the welfare of Canada than I could do for it as Prime Minister'.[32]

Thus in spite of the troubled nature of Canada's relations with the United States and in spite of suffering from American protectionist policies, Canada had one huge advantage that contemporary transitional states do not have – contiguity with the world's best market along thousands of miles of border. In the late twentieth century elaborate international negotiations, sometimes bilateral but more often multilateral, and requiring sanction from the International Monetary Fund and the World Bank, are necessary before progress can be made on trade and investment issues which will secure the kind of growth Canada enjoyed during its first hundred years. Canada lived alongside the United States leviathan and suffered for it but Canada also benefited in terms of American markets, American investment in Canada, Canadian investment in the United States, infrastructural sharing and general bilateral economic interaction.[33]

Finally, the Canadian case raises the issue of the importance of overt ideology in making democracy work. Those Canadian leaders who were successful in their own times eschewed ideology and the articulation of a national vision as an always divisive force in Canada. The question to be raised is whether it helps if leaders articulate ideological constructs round which a population can rally, or whether the fissures in most societies are so deep and intractable that the best route is the old Canadian one of simply trying to keep such issues off the active agenda. The question is a pervasive one in the contemporary world. It was put in its starkest terms when Aleksander Solzhenitsyin recently berated the Russian Parliament for its preoccupation with graft, expediency and partyism and proposed instead that the way forward should be based on a Russian ethno-centrist ideology.[34] In current circumstances most leaders in Russia and elsewhere in Central Europe are opting for the more pragmatic route while all the time hearing alarming noises off-stage from nationalist ideologues.

Leaders in all states attempting the transition to democracy are faced with similar choices. Vision is needed to inspire people, to ask them to endure hardship in difficult economic times, to help them believe in the beneficence of the state and, more problematically, the nation. But people are sceptical of such efforts. They are sceptical partly because of the point mentioned earlier, a general lack of faith in progress. They are also sceptical because of the resurgence in the late twentieth century of faith in ethnic identities, sub-state nationalisms, and regional loyalties. Using the Canadian case as an example, the technique of eschewing too clear an ideological definition of the state and the nation worked from the 1840s to the 1950s because of the economic pay off, over the long haul, which Canadian people enjoyed. The loyalty to the colonial state (differently configured in Quebec and English Canada) did not need to be created *de novo* in Canada and drew much of its sustenance from the general British imperial culture of the era. It is telling to note that in the more testing times of the last half of the twentieth century, with the rise of modern nationalism in Quebec, and the fragmenting of loyalty to traditional symbols of Canadian nationalism, these old methods have proved to be inadequate.

Political leaders in less fortunate parts of the world do not have the luxury of choice that Canadian leaders have had throughout most of Canada's history and must try to construct nationalist or federalist state ideologies which will give voters some immediate evidence that it is worth belonging to the polity and that their children and grandchildren will be better off if the new democratic system survives. Without economic payoff it is doubtful if such rhetoric will do anything except buy time. But perhaps that is the vital role for this generation of leaders to play, to buy time and hold tenuous attachments to the new states long enough for economic growth to take hold. Looking at Canadian leadership in this comparative context brings out the point that politicians used strategies in pursuit of democratic power which would now be considered as corrupt. However, the manner in which power shifted from governor-controlled executives to party leaders in the 1790–1850 period had legitimized use of patronage and influence. Political leaders were also helped by generally favourable economic conditions and by opportunities made available by territorial and administrative expansion. One great lesson offered by the Canadian case is that political leaders who succeed when democracy is in its initial stages are usually not saints.

NOTES

1. Andrew Stark, 'English Canadian Opposition to Quebec Nationalism', in R. Kent Weaver (ed.), *The Collapse of Canada*, (Brookings Institution, Washington, DC), p.127.
2. *Maclean's*, 2 Nov. 1992, p.12.
3. Mary Janigan, 'Shaping the Future', *Maclean's*, 3 July 1989, quoting Thomas Courchene, Director of the School of Policy Studies at Queen's University.
4. Ron Graham, *One Eyed Kings. Promise and Illusion in Canadian Politics* (Toronto: Collins, 1986), pp.435–6. It is worth pointing out in defence of Mulroney that he understood that Quebec's exclusion from the 1982 patriation of the 1867 British North America Act was a constitutional problem that required attention. His policy of opening up negotiations was therefore an act of statesmanship whatever other motives can be identified as tainting the enterprise.

5. *The New York Times*, 7 Nov. 1992.
6. M.Crozier, S.P. Huntington and J. Watanuki, *The Crisis of Democracy* (New York: New York University Press, 1975); Richard Rose and Guy Peters, *Can Government Go Bankrupt?* (New York: Basic Books, 1978); Samuel Brittain, *The Economic Contradictions of Democracy* (London: Temple Smith, 1977); Jurgen Habermass, *Legitimation Crisis* (Boston, MA: Beacon Press, 1975). Ernest Gellner's recent assessment of the history of civil society, *Conditions of Liberty: Civil Society and Its Rivals* (London: Hamish Hamilton, 1994), suggests the fragility of the social conditions within which democracy can flourish.
7. Arend Lijphart, *Democracy in Plural Societies: a Comparative Explanation* (New Haven, CT: Yale University Press, 1977). Application of Lijphart's approach to the Canadian case is best approached through the work of Kenneth Macrae in his two books: *Conflict and Compromise in Multilingual Societies* (Waterloo,Ontario: Wilfrid Laurier University Press, 1983) and *Consociational Democracy.Political Accommodation in Segmented Societies* (Toronto: McClelland & Stewart, 1974).
8. Macdonald's career, his impact on Canadian political culture and his view of the British North America Act can be assessed in a range of books and articles. The most sympathetic portrayal is Donald G. Creighton's two volume biography *The Young Politician, The Old Chieftain* (Toronto: Macmillan, 1952, 1955). The issues raised in this paper are dealt with at greater length in Gordon T. Stewart, *The Origins of Canadian Politics* (Vancouver: University of British Columbia Press, 1986) and 'John A. Macdonald's Greatest Triumph', *Canadian Historical Review*,Vol.LXIII (1982), pp.3–33. See also Peter B. Waite's *Macdonald. His Life and Times* (Toronto: McGraw Hill, 1975) and the same author's summary of current thinking on Macdonald in *Dictionary of Canadian Biography*, Vol.XII (Toronto: University of Toronto Press, 1990), pp.590–612.
9. J.M. Bliss, *Canadian History in Documents* (Toronto: Ryerson Press, 1966), p.220. Laurier's legacy is suggested by the title of Barbara Robertson's biography *Laurier:the Great Conciliator* (Toronto: Oxford University Press, 1971). Other standard interpretations are John W. Dafoe, *Laurier: A Study in Canadian Politics* (Toronto: McClelland & Stewart, 1963 [1922]) and Joseph Schull, *Laurier: The First Canadian* (New York: St. Martin's Press, 1965).
10. F.R. Scott 'WLMK', in A.J.M. Smith, *The Blasted Pine: An Anthology of Satire, Invective and Disrespectful Verse Chiefly by Canadian Writers* (Toronto: Macmillan, 1967).
11. Henri Bourassa, 'The French-Canadian in the British Empire', *The Monthly Review*, Vol.IX (Oct. 1902), pp.53–68 quoted in Carl Berger (ed.), *Imperialism and Nationalism 1884–1914: A Conflict in Canadian Thought* (Toronto: Copp Clark, 1969), p.73.
12. The best overview of the Mackenzie King period is Robert Bothwell, Ian Drummond and John English, *Canada 1900–1945* (Toronto: University of Toronto Press, 1987). The Second World War conscription issue is analysed on pp.331–5. The standard scholarly biography is H. Blair Neatby, *William Lyon Mackenzie King* (Toronto: University of Toronto Press, 1958, 1976) and a breathless, popular one which captures a certain feyness about the man is Bruce Hutchinson, *The Incredible Canadian: a Candid Portrait of William Lyon Mackenzie King* (New York: Longmans, 1953).
13. Andrew Stark, 'English Canadian Opposition to Quebec Nationalism', in Weaver (ed.), *The Collapse of Canada*, pp.128–34.
14. The change came during the Quiet Revolution of the 1960's when nationalists feared that if current trends continued Quebec would gradually become more and more anglophone, especially in the business world and the workplace, unless measures were taken to make French by law the working language of the province. A flavor of the times can be gained from Raymond Barbeau's *Le Québec bientôt unilingue?* (Montreal: Editions de l'homme, 1965). An informative survey of the evolution of nationalist ideology and politics since the 1960s is provided in Alain Gagnon, *Quebec: Beyond the Quiet Revolution* (Scarborough: Nelson Canada, 1990).
15. Trudeau's career is treated in Walter Stewart, *Shrug: Trudeau in Power* (Toronto: New Press, 1971), Richard J. Gwyn, *The Northern Magus: Pierre Trudeau and Canadians* (Toronto: McClelland & Stewart, 1980) and Stephen Clarkson, *Trudeau and our Times* (Toronto: McClelland & Stewart, 1990). His ideas on Canadian nationalism are dealt with in James

Laxer, *The Liberal Idea of Canada: Pierre Trudeau and the Question of Canada's Survival* (Toronto: J. Lorimer, 1977) and the origins of the fault lines that developed between him and Quebec nationalists in the 1960s are described in Gerard Pelletier's *Years of Impotence 1950–1966* (Toronto: Methuen, 1984).

16. David Milne, *Tug of War: Ottawa and the Provinces under Trudeau and Mulroney* (Toronto: J. Lorimer, 1986), p.2.
17. Christian Dufour, *Le défi québecois* (Montreal: l'Hexagone, 1989), p.13.
18. Bernard Bailyn, *The Origins of American Politics* (New York: Knopf, 1968) and Jack P. Greene, *The Quest for Power; the Lower Houses of Assembly in the Southern Royal Colonies 1689–1776* (Chapel Hill, NC: University of North Carolina Press, 1963) are the seminal works on this topic.
19. This is one of the key variables Martin Shefter indentifies as affecting the extent to which patronage takes hold in new democracies. See his 'Party and Patronage: Germany, Italy and England', *Politics & Society*, Vol.7, No.4, pp.403–51.
20. Stewart, 'John A. Macdonald's Greatest Triumph', p.21; Norman Ward', 'Responsible Government', *Journal of Canadian Studies*, Vol.XIV (1979), p.3; Alain-G. Gagnon (ed.), *Democracy with Justice* (Ottawa: Carleton University Press, 1992), pp.157–73. Stewart, *The Origins of Canadian Politics, passim*.
21. Jeffrey Simpson, *The Spoils of Power: The Politics of Patronage* (Toronto: Collins, 1988) written by the then national political correspondent of *The Globe & Mail* is a comprehensive examination of the role of patronage in Canadian politics. Ralph Heintzman, 'The Political Culture of Quebec 1840–1960', *Canadian Journal of Political Science*, Vol.XVI (1983), pp.3–59 makes the case that 'Quebec's traditional political culture was shaped by the dialectic of patronage. Economic need encouraged Québecois to exploit the political process for advancement. The result was the preoccupation of the political process with patronage'.
22. Fred W. Gibson, *Cabinet Formation and Bicultural Relations. Seven Case Studies*, Studies of the Royal Commission on Bilingualism and Biculturalism, (Ottawa: The Queen's Printer, 1970), p.171.
23. Linda Colley, *Britons: Forging the Nation 170—1837* (New Haven, CT: Yale University Press, 1992), *passim*. The conceptual starting point for Colley is taken from Benedict Anderson, *Imagined Communities:Reflections on the Origins and Spread of Nationalism* (London: Verso, 1983).
24. Jacques Monet, *The Last Cannon Shot:a Study of French Canadian Nationalism 1837–1850* (Toronto: University of Toronto Press, 1969).
25. After a period of neglect stretching back to the 1960s, when Canadian historical scholarship was shaped by the celebratory nationalism of the centennial, the case that the empire was a basis for Canadian cohesion in the nineteenth century has been recently restated by Phillip Buckner in his presidential address to the CHA in 1993: 'Whatever Happened to the British Empire', *Journal of the Canadian Historical Association*, Vol.4 (1993), pp.3–31.
26. Alan Cairns has insightful commentary on the functioning of the Canadian government in modern, fragmented society in 'The Embedded State: State–Society Relations in Canada', in Keith Banting (ed.), *State and Society: Canada in Comparative Perspective* (Toronto: University of Toronto Press, 1986), pp.53–86.
27. *The Guardian Weekly*, 9 Oct. 1994, p.12.
28. *The Globe & Mail*, 5 Jan. 1994, p.3.
29. J.H. Plumb, *The Growth of Political Stability in England 1675–1725* (London: Macmillan, 1967); W.A. Speck, *Stability and Strife. England 1714–1760* (Cambridge, MA: Harvard University Press, 1979).
30. Creighton, *John A. Macdonald. The Old Chieftan*, pp.213–42.
31. *The Economist*, Vol.333, 29 Oct. 1994, pp.55–6, 67–8.
32. Pierre de Boal to John D. Hickerson, Ottawa, 15 April 1933, Department of State, Decimal File 1930–39, Box 3179, RG59, National Archives, Washington, DC.
33. Gordon T. Stewart, *The American Response to Canada since 1776* (East Lansing, MI: Michigan State University Press, 1992), pp.175–205.
34. *The New York Times*, 30 Nov. 1994.

Democracy in Mexico

GEORGE PHILIP

This article attempts to answer three sets of questions relevant to the democratic transition in Mexico. It explores the character of the past (and to some extent present) authoritarian system. It asks whether and to what extent democratic transition is actually underway in Mexico. Finally, it seeks to relate political change to the economic transformation in that country over the past decade. The approach which the article takes is primarily historical, and political stability is explained in terms of the ability of the political elite to adapt flexibly to changing social and economic conditions. The article also raises the issue of whether the political elite would be willing to accept a transition to full-scale democracy with all its attendant uncertainties. It concludes by asking whether the devaluation of December 1994 might finally have undermined the ability of the ruling party to maintain public support.

Mexico raises some intriguing questions for students of democratic transitions. Here, we focus on three of them. One has to do with the character of the existing authoritarianism which has, after all, been exercised for many years in what is now a secular, largely urbanized and partly industrialized country- and a member of NAFTA as well. An important recent study of democratic transitions points out that, until recently, 'Mexico has never had any period of democratic rule'.[1] How has non-democracy worked in Mexico for so long? A part of the answer lies in the ability of the rulers of Mexico to make their system look more open than it is. The Mexican Constitution appears democratic and elections are held regularly. However, as has been pointed out in many places, behind the facade of democracy lie the key authoritarian institutions – the all-powerful presidency and the hegemonic ruling party.[2]

The second question is about democratic transition. Is this now taking place in Mexico, and if so how can we tell? Because Mexican authoritarianism lies behind a facade of democracy, it may be that any democratic transition need not involve a democratic rupture as such. It may simply be a matter of honouring democratic procedures by observing them better. For this reason, it is sometimes difficult in Mexico to know exactly what is changing and what is not. My own judgement is that Mexico is not yet clearly a democracy but that there is at last reason to believe that it may be on the way to becoming one.

Finally there is the difficult relationship between democratization (sometimes referred to as political modernization) and economic development (sometimes referred to as economic modernization). The traumas occasioned by the devaluation of December 1994 show that this is very much a live issue. It has been argued elsewhere, not least by this author[3] that free market economics can work well alongside democracy in Latin America. However, the relationship between economic management and democratic transition may be significantly different from the situation prevailing when countries which are already under democratic rule seek to adopt principles of free market economics.

Mexican Authoritarianism

Although authoritarian, the Mexican system shares one feature with the institutionalized democracies of the United States and Britain – namely that the past two generations have seen a broad institutional continuity. In the case of Mexico, this continuity has come at a time of major socio-economic change and other developments which might have been expected to threaten political stability.

This political stability may well have stemmed from the flexibility given to the ruling elite from the facade character of the Mexican system. Mexico has, and has had since 1917, a Constitution which looks formally democratic. There is an elected President with a six-year term of office, a Congress, elected state governors and state legislatures, and a formally-autonomous judicial power. Yet it is common ground that the system does not work in the manner that a naive interpretation of the Constitution might lead one to suppose.

Until recently at any rate, the chief impediments to democracy have been a lack of transparency in the electoral process, a lack of accountability on the part of power-holders and the overpowering influence of the executive on the whole process of government. In theory there are contested elections. Since 1940 there has always been at least one officially-recognized opposition party eligible to present candidates for election. However in practice this fact has not been especially important. In presidential elections held between 1940 and 1982 either no opposition candidate stood at all, or else the candidate of the official party (the PRI) was declared the winner by a wide margin. Sometimes the lack of serious electoral contestation ensured that the official result was plausible – if one discounts the 'anticipated reactions' effect and the many obstacles placed in the way of opposition politics. On other occasions when there were genuinely contested elections (notably 1940 and 1952), the official results are generally acknowledged to be fictitious.[4]

At state level, where the number of genuine contests has been greater, rigging was until 1989 the invariable response to contestation. In 1989, for the first time, an opposition candidate was declared the winner in a state governorship election in Mexico. Since then there have been a limited number of opposition victories, but there have been (and remain) suspicions that there is still a considerable amount of electoral malpractice in particular areas. In the mid-1990s it seems that the principle of electoral contestation has been accepted in the more developed and urbanized northern regions of Mexico, but this is not yet evidently true of the poorer and more rural south.

The 1988 Presidential elections were path-breaking in that they were contested seriously and, although the PRI was controversially declared the winner, the outcome was not totally rigged according to a predetermined pattern. In the end the PRI was declared the winner with some 50.9 per cent of the vote. While it is fairly clear that this figure was assisted by some degree of fraud, it did at least indicate a tacit admission on the part of the PRI that the opposition enjoyed real popular support. The 1988 elections were also the first presidential contest in which the ruling party accepted defeat in several states within Mexico.

The 1994 elections, too, were contested and this time the result seems to have been genuine. In the event the PRI candidate won the presidency with around one-half of the vote. By way of contrast with 1988, the PRI carried every state in Mexico although it did concede defeat in the significant Monterrey conurbation. The improved performance by the PRI in 1994 can convincingly be attributed to the improved economic record in the short-term, and the resulting popularity of the Salinas government (1988–94) – however much this has subsequently been undermined by the devaluation and revelations about several dramatic assassinations which occurred toward the end of the Salinas presidency.

One possible conclusion to draw from this is that the PRI has continued to enjoy considerable support from Mexican public opinion. Force and fraud have not always been absent from Mexican elections, but they are far from providing a complete explanation of the PRI's dominance. By the same token opposition parties, so far at least, have enjoyed no more than a very limited base of bedrock electoral support although they have been able to do very much better when capitalizing on protest votes at times of economic hardship. This last factor may be increasingly significant following the devaluation of December 1994.

Another electoral factor which has so far limited the success of the opposition parties has been the 'first past the post' system in force for presidential and gubernatorial elections. There are several opposition parties, and the PRI's ability to use its majority to change the electoral law gives it an opportunity to 'divide and rule'. For example, after the relatively strong showing by the left-wing Cuautehmoc Cardenas in 1988 the electoral laws were changed to make it very difficult for loose 'coalition' parties to take the field. For any party to be recognized, it had to run a full slate of candidates for all significant elective offices. The result was to encourage a plethora of opposition candidates to run in 1994 and to compete with each other rather than uniting against the PRI. The PRI could actually have won the election quite easily with 40 per cent of the vote – instead of the 50 per cent which it actually achieved. The laws have now been changed again in order to make official recognition more difficult for opposition parties in order to reduce their number.

The second factor mentioned above, lack of accountability, is also significant. Apart from the question of governability as such, the very relaxed legal standards which prevail in Mexico give the PRI an advantage over the opposition in competing for the popular vote – even when this is honestly counted. To some extent there are advantages which are likely to accrue in any system to a political party with a consistent record of electoral victory. For one thing, the PRI has access to resources which dwarf those available to the opposition. These resources include personnel, since the most promising and ambitious younger Mexicans rarely ally themselves willingly with the opposition. There is also the question of money. Financial information about the PRI is hard to obtain, but there is no doubt that the PRI has far more cash than the opposition parties. Then the media itself, particularly television, normally seeks to represent the PRI in a good light – in the belief that the media barons themselves will benefit from the good offices of a government which they themselves support. In fact during the 1994 election campaign Jorge Carpizo, the Interior Minister, met the head of the most important television channel (Televisa) and urged him to give more coverage to the opposition candidates. Televisa's support for the government had been so effusive until then as to constitute an embarrassment.

As this last example indicates, the relationship between the ruling party and the government is intimate and overlapping. Mexico does not have a professional civil service, and a combination of clientelism and secretive budgeting gives the authorities considerable freedom of manoeuvre when dealing with social problems or opposition demands. The judiciary was, until Zedillo's reforms at the end of 1994, generally considered to be weak and under presidential domination. Congress is still a tame institution. Public administration, electoral politics and personal favouritism could therefore easily be co-ordinated behind the closed walls of an all-powerful executive branch of government.

A further key feature of the Mexican system is the strength of the presidential institution. This is partly a matter of centralized financial control. Although there are some local taxes, and some money is released to state governors, the real financial power remains in Mexico City. The local branches of government ministries, or in some cases nationalized industries, generally win confrontations with state governors.[5] In any case, state governors can be required to resign by presidential demand. This happened so often under the Salinas administration that only a minority of governors completed their term. Furthermore such legal restraints on Presidential power as have existed, for example the budgetary process, have at times been ignored when they have proved inconvenient.[6]

There are other factors which strengthen presidential power. For one thing there is a rule that many office-holders may not be re-elected for a second term. This rule was designed to prevent corrupt politicians using incumbency to distort electoral competition. However, when applied to Congressmen and state governors the effect of this rule has often been perverse. It has prevented, or at least inhibited, the development of worthwhile relationships between voters and elected politicians. The latter become more creatures of the centre than parts of any system of checks and balances. Thus a state governor typically has more to lose by annoying central power holders than to gain by pleasing local people. He cannot threaten to resign from the PRI and run as an independent and he can be dismissed by the incumbent president at half-an-hour's notice. 'Maverick' politicians with a strictly limited regional base do nevertheless exist in Mexico, but the PRI machine is used to reward conformity and discourage excessive independence. Political discipline is relatively easy to enforce within a party which regularly wins the vast majority of elections.

The *destape*, the means by which the nomination for the PRI presidential candidate is made, further strengthens presidential power. Effectively the outgoing President makes this choice. It is true that the choice, once made, cannot be revoked. This means that there is a genuine and effective time-constraint on the power of any individual figure. Presidents serve once and once only: ex-presidents are no longer as powerful as they were. The dramatic confrontation between President Zedillo and Ex-President Salinas in February 1995, which broke out when Zedillo ordered the arrest of Salinas' brother on suspicion of murder, seems to have been resolved when the ex-president left the country. However, the key point is that ambitious Cabinet ministers need to keep the confidence of the president in the hope that this will carry them to the presidency in due course.

The majority of foreign observers of Mexico[7] have characterized the political system as authoritarian-presidentialist. Others have claimed to see subterranean forces at work within the political system which to some extent limit the political power of the president of the day. My own belief, clearly, is that the Mexican political system is authoritarian presidentialist, although this still leaves room for a broader pluralism within civil society in which powerful business interests and some intellectual influences also feature.

Democracy in Mexico?

Before considering whether this authoritarian system is slowly transforming itself into something more democratic, we need to look briefly at the nature of Mexican political society. In this context it becomes clear that there are important power resources outside the (narrowly defined) political system. Mexico may have an authoritarian system of government, but society as a whole is not obviously conformist. Presidential power is to this extent limited. When a president impinges too much on civil society or seriously misjudges a policy issue, then he is likely to face a powerful negative reaction. The political system itself may be relatively simple, but Mexican society as a whole is very complex and in some important ways resistant to political control.

Mexico is also a developing – but in some ways quite sophisticated – capitalist economy with a close and at times dependent relationship with the United States. Washington has several times within the last dozen years or so come to the Mexican government's financial rescue when crises have threatened. The NAFTA agreements are also significant restraints on the freedom of action of any Mexican government. There can be little doubt that private Mexican business interests are also very influential[k] and have become more so over time. There was introduced in 1987 a formal system of round-table negotiations between government, business and labour in which societal demands are seriously considered – though Pacted agreements can always be ignored in a crisis, as happened in December 1994.

It is clear that the main independent sources of power in Mexico come from forces which may be broadly defined as elite. The nature and behaviour of these independent forces can also be predicted to some extent from 'structural' analysis. Clearly capitalists may be expected to be powerful in a developing capitalist economy. By the same token any developing country with a 2,000 km frontier with the United Sates will face some constraints on freedom of action arising from that quarter. On a lesser but not trivial note, Mexico has a vigorous intellectual life and a widely-read print media. Governments which care about their reputation have to make some concessions to their intellectual critics.

Harder to find is evidence of the power capabilities of poorer Mexicans. There are trade unions but these are not fully independent. They are also very moderate. While they should not be seen as simple expressions of a corporate state, they are certainly not major threats to any government or public policy.[9] For the many Mexicans who are not organized, the ability to influence public policy is lesser still. However, the role of political violence, largely discounted by many observers after the failure of the 1970s guerrilla movements, has returned to centre stage with the Chiapas rising which flared briefly in January 1994 before settling down to a phoney war. There can be no doubt that the government has sufficient physical force at its disposal to defeat the insurgents, but negotiations are seen as preferable in view of the economic and reputational costs attached to a policy of coercion.

If the system just described is scarcely a brutal dictatorship, it is not especially democratic either. Rueschemeyer *et al.* point out that Mexico's 'democratic record is clearly below what one would expect on the basis of the country's level of development'.[10] Yet the Mexican system does have real support within civil society despite this lack of democracy. This support cannot easily be explained just in terms of poverty and underdevelopment. In order to consider the prospects for transformation, we need first to understand the reasons for stability.

Inevitably, we start with the legacy of the Revolution and earlier historical episodes. Mexican history until 1920 was a series of violent upheavals, inconclusively settled. Even under Spanish rule, there were a large number of conflicts and risings: scholars still do not really understand why.[11] The war of independence itself was long and bloody and, tragically, failed to resolve key issues of internal power. As a result the nineteenth century saw a number of civil wars and conflicts. This was also a disastrous period for Mexico in that it lost much of its national territory to the United States, and also endured a period of foreign occupation under Maximilian. According to some scholar, Mexican per capita income was around one-quarter of that of the United States in 1820: by 1870 the ratio had widened to around 14:1.[12] The Mexican Revolution, the last and greatest of the upheavals in that country's history, took place between 1910 and 1917. Around one million people died, mostly of famine and disease, from a total population of 14 million.

The Mexican Revolution was a complex affair. It was neither a simple social movement nor principally an ideological one.[13] It certainly had radical and reformist implications, and should not just be seen as a violent upheaval. Certain exclusionary ideologies were overthrown and social forces defined as reactionary (the Church, the established military, the landed elite) were defeated. In their place the Revolutionaries put at least a promise of national unity.

Mexican history, therefore, offers several legacies which help to explain contemporary institutions. One of them is a violent and difficult past. This is something from which the ideals of peace, order, national unity and development held out the possibility of escape. Another legacy is the allegiance claimed by memory of the glorious Revolution itself. The PRI is still, nominally, the party of the Revolution. Somewhat less nominally, it does genuinely see itself as the party of national unity. In a society which is (still) to a degree ethnically stratified, this unifying appeal is no trivial influence and it commands some real support. Yet another legacy is the continuing corporatist control over labour and other subordinate classes, which dates from the days when the state was interested in mobilising the masses rather than keeping them quiet in the interests of economic growth.

In any event the characteristics of the post-1940 Mexican state were a primary concern with discipline and order, and with economic development. Development was sought by essentially capitalist means, through with some important specific nuances designed to cope with the peculiarities of the Mexican situation. A few symbolic gestures to social reform and economic nationalism were also made, but these were by no means the dominant trends of the time.

There can be no doubt that the political climate has changed greatly since the high point of Mexican authoritarianism was reached in the 1960s, but there may be disagreement about how much. In my own judgement, the Mexican system did become significantly more liberal between 1970 and the mid 1980s, though not noticeably more democratic. The last decade has seen more genuine contestation for power, but the transition to democracy is not yet complete.

Some of the pressures for more political openness which developed in the late 1960s can be understood easily enough from a 'modernization' perspective. Mexico's population and living standards both increased fairly rapidly during 1940–70. The result was a much larger urban population – probably just a majority by 1970 – and a much larger middle class. The size of the student population also increased. However, the political system itself, rather simple and authoritarian in concept, did not modernize in conjunction with the modernization of society. By the same token, the 'Malthusian' combination of a rising population and a fixed amount of land created increasing difficulties for the rural corporatist institutions which had both controlled and in some respects assisted the Mexican peasantry. Despite the extensive land reforms of the 1930s, the system had no easy answer to a growing population of rural poor who lacked access to enough land to make a living.

It should be noted, however, that the Mexican student movement of the late 1960s, like its counterpart in the developed democracies, was not self-consciously in favour of what many of its supporters would have considered 'bourgeois' democracy. Its expressed values were far more communal and socialist. It was therefore open to the reformists within the system to seek to co-opt student radicals by changing policies rather than reforming the system itself.

Later critics claimed, in fact, that the 1970s governments adopted misconceived policies of social reform instead of the democratic reforms which the situation required.[14] Nevertheless, while change at the centre of power took place only slowly, the system did become markedly less authoritarian in its treatment of dissidence and opposition. The 'spirit of 1968' continued to exist in opposition periodicals and minority parties of the Left. The political reform of 1977 gave a greater measure of freedom to both of these. It would be too much to say that the Left opposition was able to mount a serious challenge to the system, but it did contribute toward the development of a less deferential and more critical attitude to those in authority. The tone of public life became far less authoritarian as a result.[15]

The government also faced increased opposition from the political Right. There had been since 1939 a (relatively limited) semi-Catholic opposition concentrated on the PAN. After 1982 the PAN was able to take advantage of a period of government unpopularity to increase its share of the vote considerably. By the mid-1980s it could mount an effective challenge to the PRI in a number of states, though it was clearly not yet a contender for power at the national level.

The outcome of all of this was to increase the amount of contestation within Mexican politics, but only within certain limits. Indeed there were several occasions when it looked as though the official party might allow a serious challenge for power. These was especially true of the period 1983–84.[16] Eventually, however, the regime showed that it would not accept electoral defeat except on the most trivial scale. Opposition electoral victories were either not accepted, or were quickly reversed. After some important local elections were spectacularly rigged in 1985 and 1986, it became clear that Mexico was as authoritarian as ever.

Since around 1986, however, the political system has faced a further set of challenges to which it is still struggling to respond. One key event was a split in the ruling party in 1986, which greatly if temporarily strengthened the Left. We have already seen that the 1988 presidential elections were (by Mexican standards) closely contested. There were also a series of dramatic developments during 1994 and early 1995, the significance of which is still to be evaluated. There seems little doubt, however, that the key explanations for the rapid changes under way in Mexico do not relate simply to its social modernization (though this is a background factor which should not be ignored) but also to the way in which government policies have interacted with economic and social change. The key question which has now to be faced is whether the pattern of economic development sought by the Mexican authorities – which involves close economic integration with the

United States via the NAFTA and other institutions – is compatible with maintaining a political system which has in the past shown itself to be authoritarian, secretive and very suspicious of outsiders. On the other hand, there are undoubtedly ways in which rapid economic change (not always for the better) is making democratic reform more difficult. In order to put these questions in context, we need to move on to consider the relationship between political change and economic development (such as it has been) in Mexico.

Political vs. Economic 'Modernization'?

Until the 1930s Mexico's society, and economy, were principally agrarian. Living standards were low and life expectancy short. Frequent violent upheavals had largely aborted any sustained rise in living standards. From around the late 1930s, however, signs of material improvement became manifest. These continued throughout the 1940s and 1950s. A striking feature of this period of growth was that agriculture expanded alongside industry.[17] After around 1965 the rate of agricultural growth slowed. Some degree of policy error may have been involved here, but the overall trend was probably inevitable due to the complex pressures of Mexican social geography and competition from hightech North American agriculture. By the mid-1960s the Mexican population had doubled from its 1940 level, and policies of raising agricultural productivity and extending irrigation could not in the end keep pace. However, the agrarian question is complex, and some scholars have argued that the authorities – as a result of ideological bias toward capitalist individualism – did not provide enough help to the collectively-run agriculture which operated in many regions of Mexico.[18]

The 1940–65 period was also one of rapid industrialization based on the home market. Industrial growth was facilitated by a trade surplus earned by export agriculture and later by tourism. Government policy was fairly *laissez-faire* except for a general bias towards protectionism. Fiscal policy was orthodox with price stability a major objective. Unusually for Latin America, the peso held its value against the dollar between 1954 and 1976.

These trends, although positive in many ways, became a source of some concern to policy-makers as the 1960s wore on. The main problems with the growth pattern were growing inequality, a relatively declining agriculture, and fears of a fiscal crisis since pressures on public spending could not easily be contained.[19] Meanwhile the political leadership, especially under the rather rigid administration of Diaz Ordaz (1964–70), had no answer to the rising expectations of parts of the urban middle class. The student unrest of 1968 led to the Tlatelolco massacre, when soldiers fired on a student demonstration. Scholars began to argue that the Mexican system was authoritarian, capitalist and increasingly divisive between the rich and poor.[20] Some political insiders, conscious of the gap between the promises of the Revolution and the realities of late 1960s Mexico, tended to agree.

After around 1970 the Mexican state sought to resolve the country's difficulties by an aggressive policy of increasing public spending. This was financed by a combination of foreign debt and oil income. This combination, clearly, was possible only because large-scale oil discoveries were made in Mexico in and after 1972 and because the international banks were keen to lend petrodollars to many developing countries. Nevertheless the decision to pursue oil-financed and debt-financed 'development' was made principally for domestic reasons – with just a hint of pressure from the United States. The 1974–81 period was one of rapidly rising oil production and consequent euphoria. However, these policies proved unsustainable because public spending and imports during this period increased even more rapidly than oil revenue and exports. The Lopez Portillo government's attempt to recapture the initiative by nationalizing the banks in September 1982 only added a further dimension to the crisis. At the end of 1982 Mexico had $100 billion of foreign debt, inflation in triple digits, a declining economy, no private sector confidence whatever, and a frustrated population wondering where the oil money had gone.

The 1982 crisis left Mexican policy-makers looking for a new impetus for renewed economic growth. It did take some time for the magnitude of the crisis to sink in. De la Madrid, who took office as president in December 1982, at first believed that nothing more radical was required than an ordinary IMF-type adjustment programme and that economic growth would soon resume as normal. The need to reorient the entire economy, mooted only on the fringes of official Mexico in 1982–84, only became clear when the price of oil crashed at the end of 1985.

Meanwhile Washington, preoccupied with problems in Central America, was slow to attend to the potentially far more serious issue of Mexico. And the banks, privately more aware of the problems, were desperate to prevent any outright debt default until they could find a way to protect themselves from its worst consequences. There was a short period in which Latin American debt problems threatened to overwhelm the whole international banking system and short-term expedients inevitably tended to overshadow long-term thinking.

When the 1982 shock was compounded by the sharp fall in the oil price which took place during 1985–86, it finally became clear to the Mexican authorities that they needed to restructure their economy in a radical way. Economic restructuring, towards manufacturing exports and away from dependency on oil, involved the government in a search for different strategic alliances with civil society.

The government at first sought to limit the amount of change required by confining its commitment to reform to the narrowly-defined economic field. Government spokesmen carefully rehearsed the formula 'economic reform now, political reform later' and in practice felt the need to consolidate the ruling coalition at a time of growing stress and uncertainty. This was not a climate in which political pluralism was welcome. The government used its own supply of dollars earned from oil to help some of the private sector companies worst hit by the devaluation: political loyalty was a prerequisite for help of this kind. Electoral opposition was not welcomed either. In 1985 and 1986 state governorship election results in the north of Mexico were spectacularly rigged. We do not know what the real voting results were, but the PRI's attitude was such that it would have demanded victory even if it had managed scarcely a vote in its favour.[21]

From 1986, however, there was a progressive linking between the Mexican economy and that of the United States. The Baker Plan of 1986 was the first systematic effort to help Latin American countries with debt problems.[22] It was fairly limited in scope, but was eventually followed by the more ambitious Brady Plan and subsequently by Mexico's adherence to the NAFTA. The US Treasury was again brought into play following the assassination of Donaldo Colosio in March 1994 and the post-devaluation crisis of 1994–95.

The consequences of this economic re-orientation were (and are) complex. One significant development was that the Mexican government was able to win political support from the private sector in return for a far more aggressive approach to market-oriented reform than it had shown until then. The Mexican industrial elite – which was extremely disturbed by the 1982 crisis and the bank nationalization – essentially agreed to support the existing political system with only limited reform in return for a radical change in economic orientation. The business elite was certainly content enough with the notion of 'economic reform now, political reform later'.

One of the resulting changes was the recognition, by the Mexican state, of independent business associations which had previously been very critical of government policy. These associations then negotiated hard for meaningful market-oriented reform with measures which included accelerated privatization and a reduction in the role of the state. Since 1987, when the first of a series of 'economic pacts' was announced between government, business and the official unions, big business has generally been regarded as a partner of government with a legitimate input into the making of public policy. The policies themselves have been free market-oriented and geared to closer economic relations with the United States.

Washington itself was involved in Mexican government policy-making earlier and with less overt resistance than was the case with Mexican

business. Since 1982 there has been a distinct change in the pattern of
negotiations with the United States. At the beginning economic negotiations
were largely restricted to crisis management. The Reagan administration
was willing to offer limited help to Mexico at the deepest point of the
financial crisis, but its own cold war concerns prevented it from taking any
very great interest in the detail of Mexican economic policy. Later
Washington's involvement deepened as it became clear that Mexico could
not on its own recover from the crisis. The Baker Plan of 1986 was a
significant change of US policy. The Brady Plan of 1989, which offered a
reduction in Mexican foreign debt in return for the acceptance of free
market policies, was a further step toward even closer relationships. The
NAFTA agreement took the transition further still. Mexico, the United
States and Canada are now regular and legally-established economic
partners with certain specific rights and duties toward each other. The fresh
bail-out of the Mexican economy during 1994–95 added a further variation
to an old theme.

The Mexican elite, which in the 1970s contained some nationalist
elements, has now been recomposed around three semi-fixed points. The
government is run by foreign (principally US) trained technocrats, whose
primary motivation is the desire to bring economic development to Mexico.
Big business strongly approves. Both of these groups see no alternative to
closer integration with the United States, which is seen as a necessary (if not
especially desired) means to this end. Finally, the United States government,
and US business, also supports policies of free market economics and
integration with the United States.

It is too early to say whether this new development project is likely to
work. The devaluation of December 1994 was a real setback. What is clear,
however, is that the PRI has transformed itself from a post-revolutionary
party with a strong nationalist identity to a moderate pro-capitalist party
with a more liberal public face. It is underpinned by a broader alliance
between very big business, the media barons and the technocrats in
government. It shares a common purpose which is at least as coherent as
that of any Asian NIC. Its belief, that the NAFTA and related changes offer
Mexico an unparalleled opportunity to develop economically, may well
prove accurate despite some occasional setbacks. And this elite has limited
tolerance for anything or anybody who might want to stand in the way of
what it sees as modernization.

However, capitalist states cannot dispense with the need for legitimation
because they have limited control over the market forces upon which they
depend. Constraints on the freedom of the Mexican government are
particularly evident because the keystone of the whole development
strategy – economic integration with the United States – requires American

public opinion to accept that Mexico truly is a democracy.

Yet there are some ironies here. For one thing foreign capital – particularly of the short-term kind – may prefer the idea of democracy in Mexico to democracy itself, and may be excessively concerned about short-term political risk to be very appreciative of painful, but necessary, democratizing measures – let alone democratic uncertainties. While there are relatively few general patterns evident in comparative studies of democratization, there is surely one robust conclusion that can be drawn. The process of democratic transition rarely runs smoothly. Even where it does, there is still the perception of difficulty and danger. Furthermore, democracy itself involves uncertainties and risks. However, markets dislike uncertainty, and are likely to be particularly averse to the kind which is inherent in rapid political change.

On the other hand the United States government actually needs a democratic and reasonably prosperous Mexico. Until the recent devaluation Mexico was a rapidly growing market for US exports, having just overtaken Japan to become the USA's second-largest market. The reverse side of the coin is that Mexico is also the largest supplier of illegal migrants to the United States. Since Mexicans are still producing nearly two million live births a year, the pressure of population on the Mexican ecology and economy is still growing. Washington may see the alternative to a relatively prospering Mexico as being barbed wire, border guards and an increasingly xenophobic mentality. The US government, therefore, has little choice but to help Mexico and to put the best face which it can on whatever democratic reforms the Mexican authorities see fit to carry out.

However, the strategy of capitalist integration with the United States does threaten economic hardship for very many Mexicans. Rapid economic growth may well offer the prospect of relief in the longer run, but the long run is not yet upon us. The effect of the Mexican government's free market reforms during 1987–94 was to a great extent to make the rich richer. This is not to deny that many poorer Mexicans benefited to some degree from lower inflation, better public services and a limited resumption of growth, but there can be no doubt that significant numbers felt excluded from the process. The popular resonance which greeted the Chiapas rising of January 1994 cannot be understood unless we remember that the post-1987 economic strategy adopted by the PRI is inherently divisive.

For these reasons, it has not been easy for the new elite to combine the purity of its objectives with the uncertainties of electoral politics. There have, nevertheless, been some important changes of outlook. Since 1988 there has been less ballot rigging (which is not to say none) but the PRI has sought to prevail in more open election competition by fielding a formidable array of political experience along with financial and media fire-power. The

PRI was to some degree reformed under Salinas. It became, not more democratic, but more professional. In 1988 it still had had many of the characteristics of a clientelist apparatus which was voter-repelling as much as mobilizing. For example, the PRI candidate for the Senate in Mexico City (who was close to the official labour movement) polled significantly worse than Salinas himself, who, as the PRI's presidential candidate, was heavily defeated in the capital. By 1994, however, the PRI looked far more like a political party – not perhaps a mass membership party of the European type, but at least a slick and professional organization. Fewer people became candidates of the PRI because of good contacts or long service. Ability counted for rather more. Recognition of the occasional opposition victory meant that the PRI had to fight to win, and losing candidates with limited popular appeal could be dropped. As the PRI had to take the opposition more seriously, so it offered fewer 'soft targets' to the opposition in local elections and benefited as a result.[23]

However, the PRI has tried to ring in the new without altogether abandoning the old. There is still a certain amount of electoral 'alchemy' in the poorer and more backward parts of Mexico and the PRI has not been bounded, as yet, by any significant degree of financial accountability. One of the architects of the 1994 campaign, the prominent politician and multimillionaire businessman Carlos Hank Gonzalez, was best known in Mexico for his aphorism that 'a politician who is poor is a poor politician'. Furthermore, one of the reasons for the devaluation crisis of December 1994 was the lending binge undertaken by the state development banks prior to the elections of that year.

The PRI is now, in many ways, a political party like the others but with additional advantages which are not available to the opposition. It has vastly more experience of politics and government than any opposition party. In addition, state and private resources have both been used to build support in pivotal locations. The relationship between government and official party remains close, especially at election time. There is also an electoral system which is helpful to a governing party.

By the same token, though, the PRI's advantages over the opposition parties are no longer overwhelming. They can easily be outweighed by serious governmental unpopularity as a result of economic setback or failure. The devaluation of December 1994 has therefore provided the opposition with opportunities to take advantage of the loss of Mexican prestige and living standards that has resulted. It is too early to say whether these opportunities will be fully exploited, or whether the government will continue to accept the existing rules if they lead to serious defeats. However, the course of Mexican politics suddenly looks rather different and more open than it did at the time of the 1994 elections.

The immediate prospect in Mexico is for something which looks far more like contested party competition than the rather one-sided contests in the past. Rueschemeyer *et al.* have suggested that the existence of a reasonably effective conservative party has been a key pre-requisite for successful democratic transition in South America.[24] It is likely that a transformation of the PRI into something resembling a moderate pro-capitalist party would be helpful for democratic transition.

However, there remain obstacles to a smooth democratic transition – or indeed any transition at all. It may be quite true that there are many PRIistas who could operate willingly enough in a fully democratic environment. Most of Zedillo's cabinet would be content enough to live in a full democracy. However, there is also a section of the old PRI which prefers secretiveness, authoritarianism and in some cases downright corruption to genuine democracy. The question is not so much whether this section of the PRI is any longer essential to the workings of the system (it is not) but whether it can be dismantled quietly without damage to it.

The Zedillo administration has clearly decided to do its best to uphold the law rather than protect the system's loyalists. Among his first acts in office were the reform of the Supreme Court (which was mainly a matter of replacing political hacks with trained lawyers) and the appointment of a member of the PAN as his Attorney General. The pace of events since then has been very rapid, with the spectacular arrest of Raul Salinas in March 1995.

There can be little doubt that any democratic system does depend upon a system of laws, properly upheld. At the same time many Mexicans, and some foreigners, have seen these judicial reforms (and arrests) as very threatening. Quite apart from anything else, this new-found enthusiasm for the rule of law has certainly shed a certain amount of light on aspects of the Mexican system which were previously considered to be top secret. This secrecy itself conferred advantages. One thing which capitalists tended to find attractive about Mexico was its political stability, and the enthusiasm of foreign investors for countries in which newspapers headlines are frequently dramatic can without question be exaggerated.

We should conclude this discussion by noting some more of the paradoxes at the heart of the debate about political and economic modernization. The PRI can best prove its democratic credentials by losing power, but its main motive for adopting such credentials is precisely to avoid losing. Meanwhile, the private sector wants democracy, but fears democratization. Fears of political upheaval, which are often exaggerated, are now themselves a significant factor in contributing to Mexico's present economic difficulties. These difficulties have clearly impacted upon the popularity of the PRI and increased the competitiveness of the political system. It is precisely because the coalition between the PRI, the government and the (domestic and foreign) private sector has proved shaky that real democratic reform is now on the agenda.

The Future of Mexican Politics

During the second half of 1994 there was a considerable discussion of the need for political reform. This discussion resulted from the Chiapas rising, which seriously embarrassed the government, and several assassinations which hit the headlines during 1994. However, the PRI did win the August 1994 elections convincingly, and it was not clear whether the promise of political reform was intended as more than a cosmetic exercise designed mainly to re-establish political consensus.

Incoming Mexican presidents offered what they described as political reform in 1965, 1971, 1977, 1983 and 1989 but all of these reforms proved to be either very limited, or purely cosmetic, or else they were aborted when they threatened to bring about real change. Zedillo's promises of reform seem to have been quite genuinely intended in so far as they involved more thorough enforcement of existing laws, but there was no evidence that he came to power with the deliberate intention of surrendering the dominant position still enjoyed by the PRI.

Mexico's renewed lurch into economic crisis in December 1994, combined with the Zedillo administration's dramatic break with the Salinas period, have however introduced a genuinely new factor into the whole process. Much of the old political elite (and some of the newer technocracy) is now fatally discredited. It is clear that the Salinas government's strategy of radical economic reform coupled with only limited political reform has now to be revised. Furthermore, the apparent failure of years of free market reform to improve significantly the living standards of the average Mexican must raise questions of a more profound kind. An optimist might assert that the present-day economic crisis will appear in retrospect as a kind of storm before the calm – relating more to the disequilibria inherent in economic transition than to any deep flaw in the concept of Naftonian development. Even if this is true, however, the political effect of the devaluation has given a new lease of life to opposition parties which seemed well beaten in the 1994 elections. If the optimists are wrong and present crisis is an indication that the whole development strategy is itself flawed, then the political consequences may be even more far-reaching.

It does seem clear as well that the cumulative effect of incremental changes over the past generation are at last having a combined qualitative effect on the whole nature of the system. A combination of market-oriented reform, moderate democratization and integration into the NAFTA have reduced the system's opportunities for corporatist or protectionist responses to crisis. In the past clientelistic arrangements were used widely to take the edge off local discontent. In fact this was a key means by which the turbulent revolutionary Mexico was tamed and pacified during the 1940s and 1950s. However, today clientelism is widely seen as an expensive, inefficient and unjust means of dealing with discontent. It is also seen as a possible source of arbitrary, and therefore 'illegitimate', power. Media scrutiny, a more independent and assertive judiciary and the increased difficulties with keeping secrets in Mexican politics (or indeed politics anywhere) have also contributed to reducing the advantages of arbitrary power and making successful authoritarian reaction less and less likely. Time may at last be running out for the present system.

Meanwhile, the developmental elites which are still supporting the PRI want some continuation of reform. Developmentalists are not democrats by conviction (at least not in the Mexican context), but they are opposed to overt and arbitrary authoritarianism which they see (rightly) as bad for business in a Naftonian context. Mexican business has always welcomed some forms of authoritarian control – such as the enforced moderation of the labour unions in which discipline was backed up by the closed shop and union card. But it does want protection against erratic or antagonistic political elites. It also wants to avoid the appearance of repression and civil conflict which are likely, now more than ever, to send out quite the wrong signals internationally.

In fact the political and economic elite want the legitimation provided by democracy in order to pursue economic development. At the same time some elite groups remain uneasy about the way in which genuinely open politics can introduce unpredictabilities into economic decision making. If these elite groups could enjoy democratic legitimation without the real contestation for power inherent in a democracy, they would happily accept it. But this formula now seems unattainable. It may well be that they will have to take their chances with genuine democracy instead.

NOTES

1. D. Rueschemeyer, E. Stephens and J. Stephens, *Capitalist Development and Democracy* (Cambridge: Polity Press, 1992).
2. C. Cansino, 'Mexico: The Challenge of Democracy', *Government and Opposition*, Vol.30, No.1 (1995), pp.60–73, and G. Philip, *The Presidency in Mexican Politics* (Basingstoke: Macmillan, 1992).
3. G. Philip, 'The New Economic Liberalism and Democracy in Spanish America', *Government and Opposition*, Vol.29, No.3 (1994), pp.363–77.
4. D. Cosio Villegas, *El sistema politico mexicano: las posibilidades de cambio* (Mexico City: Joaquin Mortiz, 1972).
5. C. Loret de Mola, *Confesiones de un gobernador* (Mexico City: Grijalbo, 1978).

6. J. Teichman, *Policymaking in Mexico: From Boom to Crisis* (Boston, MA: Allen & Unwin, 1988).
7. S.K. Purcell and J. Purcell, 'Must a Stable Polity be Institutionalised: The Case of Mexico', *World Politics*, 1980, pp.194–227; E. Stevens, *Protest and Response in Mexico* (Cambridge, MA: MIT Press, 1974); G. Philip, *The Presidency in Mexican Politics*.
8. M. Basazez, *La lucha por la hegemonia en Mexico* (Mexico City: Siglo XXI, 1980).
9. I. Roxborough, *Unions and Politics in Mexico: The Case of the Automobile Industry* (Cambridge: Cambridge University Press, 1984).
10. Rueschemeyer *et al.*, *Capitalist Development*, p.199.
11. F. Katz (ed.), *Riot, Rebellion and Revolution: Rural Social Conflict in Mexico* (Princeton, NJ: Princeton University Press, 1989).
12. J. Vazquez and L. Meyer, *The United States and Mexico* (Chicago, IL: University of Chicago Press, 1985).
13. A. Knight, *The Mexican Revolution* (Cambridge: Cambridge University Press, 1986).
14. R. Newall and L. Rubio, *Mexico's Dilemma: The Political Origins of Economic Crisis* (Boulder, CO: Westview Press, 1984).
15. H. Aguilar Camin, *Despues del Milagro* (Mexico City: Cal y Arena, 1988).
16. N. Cox, 'Changes in the Mexican Political System', in G. Philip (ed.), *Politics in Mexico* (London: Croom Helm, 1985).
17. A Knight, 'The Political Economy of Revolutionary Mexico' in C. Abel and C. Lewis (eds.), *Latin America: Economic Imperialism and the State* (London: Athlone Press, 1985), pp.288–317; R. Enriquez, 'The Rise and Collapse of Stabilising Development' in G. Philip (ed.), *The Mexican Economy* (London: Routledge, 1988), pp.8–40.
18. S. Sanderson, *The Transformation of Mexican Agriculture: International Structure and the Politics of Rural Change* (Princeton, NJ: Princeton University Press, 1986).
19. E.V.K. FitzGerald, 'The Financial Constraint on Relative Autonomy: The State and Capital Accumulation in Mexico, 1940–82', in C. Anglade and C. Fortin, *The State and Capital Accumulation in Latin America* (London: Macmillan, 1985).
20. An influential, English-language, version of this argument is presented in R.D. Hansen, *The Politics of Mexican Development* (Baltimore, MD: Johns Hopkins University Press, 1971).
21. A. Alvarado (ed.), *Electoral Patterns and Perspectives in Mexico* (San Diego: Center for US-Mexican Studies, 1987).
22. E. Duran, 'Mexico's 1986 Financial Rescue: Palliative or Cure?' in G. Philip (ed.), *The Mexican Economy*.
23. J. Arroyo and S. Morris, 'The Electoral Recovery of the PRI in Guadalajara, Mexico', *Bulletin of Latin American Research*, Vol.12, No.1 (1993), pp.91–103.
24. Rueschemeyer *et al.*, *Democracy and Capitalist Development*.

The Segregated State? Black Americans and the Federal Government[1]

DESMOND KING

This study examines the significance of segregated race relations in the Federal government in the decades after the election of Woodrow Wilson in 1912. It is argued that the role of the Federal government in introducing and maintaining segregation is an overlooked feature of the American state with implications for its character and for its relationship with Black Americans. Section II explains the judicial and partisan support for segregation. Section III deploys archival records to provide a detailed account of the dissemination of segregation in Federal government departments after 1913. Setion IV explains why Republican presidents and congresses in the 1920s failed to erode segregation in government departments, emphasising the growth of racism amongst white voters in Northeastern and Midwestern cities. Section V concludes the study by identifying some of the legacies of Federal support for segregated race relations.

I. Introduction

In his distingushed study of Reconstruction, Eric Foner argues that Reconstruction and the settlement of 1877 ensured the 'South's racial system remained regional rather than national'.[2] In this study I argue that this view neglects the introduction and maintenance of segregated race relations in the Federal government itself, and the effects upon public policy.[3] For Black Americans, the US Federal government was a defender of the legally sanctioned practice of segregation.[4] It tolerated segregated race relations within its own bureaucracy and in Federal programmes. In the long decades preceding the passage of the Civil Rights Act in 1964, American democracy was compromised by the presence of two classes of employees – determined by race – in its Federal offices and departments. This arrangement has implications for both the relationship between Black Americans and the Federal government and conventional theories of the American state. As the National Association for the Advancement of Colored People (NAACP), and other activists working on behalf of Black Americans, explained, segregation created second class citizenship. In August 1913, Moorfield Storey wrote from the NAACP to President Woodrow Wilson explaining this effect of segregation: 'this Government, founded on the theory of complete equality and freedom of all citizens, has established two classes among its civilian employees. It has set the colored people apart as if mere contact with them were contamination'. Furthermore, Black American employees were condemned to a dispiritingly low position in the state: 'to them is held out only the prospect of mere subordinate routine service without the stimulus of advancement to high office by merit'.[5]

It is, of course, hardly novel to remark upon the absence of complete democracy in the United States before the 1964 civil rights legislation.[6] What is less quotidian is the central role played by the Federal government itself in imposing and maintaining segregated race relations in its own institutions. This position limited fundamentally the nature of American democracy.

Segregated race relations in the Federal government were not predetermined. In the 30 years between the establishment of the Civil Service Commission (under the Pendleton Act of 1883) and the election of Woodrow Wilson to the presidency in 1913, Black Americans could realistically identify the Federal civil service – and its regional offices – as a source of employment.[7] Such applicants were treated in an equal and meritocratic way.[8] Van Riper argues that the application of merit criteria and the eschewing of photographs on application forms in the 25 years after the Pendleton Act benefited Black Americans seeking to enter the civil service: ' ... the generally impersonal nature of the examination system encouraged Negro employment, particularly in the city of Washington, and the effective entry of the Negro into the federal public service must be dated from 1883'. He highlighted the success of Black graduates:

> Especially noteworthy was the entry of numbers of graduates of the new Negro colleges and universities by 1890. At this time the Negro employees included four consuls in the State Department, a division chief in the Treasury, the recorder of Interior's General Land Office, at least three collectors of customs, and, at the top, the Hon. Blanche K Bruce, a former senator from Mississippi and the Recorder of Deeds for the District of Columbia, who was paid in fees at an estimated $18,000 a year.[9]

From 1913, these propitious circumstances changed for several reasons. First, Woodrow Wilson was elected to the White Huouse and appointed southern Democrats to Cabinet offices, many of whom were committed to segregating their departmental employees. Second, Democrats achieved control of the House of Representatives for the first time in several decades and encouraged Federal departments to segregate their workers. Third, the Civil Service Commission, in May 1914, required applicants for civil service posts to supply a photograph with their application form (a requirement rescinded only in 1940). The result of this constellation of forces was the introduction and dissemination of segregated race relations into Federal government departments.

The study is structured as follows. In section II the familiar judicial and partisan bases of support for segregated race relations are quickly sketched. Section III provides a detailed account of the introduction and dissemination of segregated arrangements in the Federal government in the years after 1913. Section IV considers why the shift to Republican presidencies and congresses between 1921 and 1932 did not result in the erosion of segregated race relations in the bureaucracy. Section V concludes the study.

II. The Politics of Segregation

Segregated race relations existed in the Federal government before the election of Woodrow Wilson in 1912, and the accompanying dominance of Democrats in Congress, but they were not widespread or encouraged by Cabinet officers. Thus the movement to segregate needs to be located in this period. There are several factors underpinning this support.

First, the Supreme Court's judgement in *Plessy v. Ferguson* in 1896 permitting the organisation of American public life in terms of 'separate but equal' arrangements imparted constitutional-legal authority to racial separation. This doctrine was resolute until the 1954 *Brown* decision, although chips to the tenet began from the late 1930s. Exploitation of the opportunities posed by 'separate but equal' restrictions was not confined to the South and southerners but occurred, to varying degrees, throughout the United States in the new century.

Second, from the first Wilson presidency, Congress became a staunch defender of segregated race relations, practices less salient though far from eroded during the Republican party's dominance in the 1920s. The Democrats' electoral success in 1912 was followed by the introduction of numerous bills into the House of Representatives proposing to segregate Black employees from whites in the Federal civil service.[10] Bill H.R. 13772 (introduced in 1914) sought to segregate Black employees from whites in the Federal government while H.R. 17541 aimed to make it unlawful for Black recruits to obtain either commissioned or non-commissioned positions in the Armed Forces.[11] H.R. 5968, introduced in 1913, proposed to 'effect certain reforms in the civil service by segregating clerks and employees of the white race from those of African blood or descent'.[12]

The upsurge in bills to segregate employees in the civil service by race with the election of Woodrow Wilson and Democratic majorities in Congress was no coincidence. Although these bills failed, their introduction and discussion in the Congress conveys the atmosphere fuelling race relations and encouraging the marginalisation of Black Americans. In 1916, hearings were held before the House Committee on the District of Columbia (chaired by Ben Johnson from Kentucky) to discuss a set of bills proposing to outlaw 'intermarriage of whites and negroes' and to require 'separate accommodations in street cars'.[13] By the 1920s, few politicians dissented publicly from the desirability of segregation and opponents lacked the political power effectively to prevent its diffusion. A robust approach to segregation was embraced by many Democrats. One Republican Senator, Theodore E Burton, responding to NAACP protests about segregation in the government, explained the partisan source of its introduction: 'you will notice that this order has been issued under a Democratic Administration'.[14] Southern Democratic Senators such as Hoke Smith of Georgia, Benjamin Tillman of South Carolina and James Vardaman of Mississippi enthusiastically exercised the new power granted them in the Sixty-First Congress (1913–14). They were active in the Democratic Fair Play Association formed, in 1913, to advance Southern Democratic interests in Washington (of which Woodrow Wilson was an honorary member). Opposing a motion appropriating funds to Black Americans to celebrate 50 years of freedom, Senator Vardaman reminded his senatorial colleagues that, 'really the white man has done more for the negro than the negro has done for himself. As a matter of fact, there is no race of people on earth who have received as much help from others as the negroes of the South have received from the white people of the South'.[15] His views were not isolated ones.

Third, Woodrow Wilson was elected to the White House in 1912 and the Democrats gained majorities in both houses of the Congress. This Democratic electoral success facilitated the segregationist propensity in Washington: '*never before has there been an Administration that dared to cater to this feeling, except in surreptitious ways*. There has always been in the Departments in Washington, a *wish* to do it, but not the *courage*'.[16] His presidency broke with the policies of his republican progressive predecessors, Theodore Roosevelt (1901–9) and William Howard Taft (1909-13).[17] The new emphasis was propelled by partisan interests. Wilson appointed Southerner supporters to Cabinet positions, some of whom attempted to entrench the Democratic Party in the Federal state, aware that his electoral success of 1912 owed everything to a split in the Republicans rather than to the extent of his own support. Democratic Party strength grew in the Congress to 291 Representatives and 51 Senators, compared with 228 and 41 under the previous Republican administration.

Woodrow Wilson seems himself to have imbibed prevailing racist attitudes and to have accepted the desirability of segregation in American life. One student of the Wilson presidency, Kendrick Clements, adopting a rather anodyine tone, accuses the Democratic President of 'insensitivity' towards Black employees.[18] The same author maintains that while Wilson subscribed to 'none of the crude, vicious racism of James K. Vardaman or Benjamin R. Tillman', he was none the less unprepared to exert himself to defend Black Americans: 'Wilson was unwilling to take even [a] small step toward changing racial relations if it might jeopardize other reforms'.[19] He also sanctioned the segregationist actions of his appointees such as William Gibbs McAdoo at the Treasury and Albert S. Burleson at the Post Office Department. Clements concludes, rightly, that 'as a result of the president's attitude racism was licensed in the federal bureaucracy more than it had been before, but practices were not uniform throughout the administration'.[20]

To justify his support of segregation Wilson cited 'national considerations', though failing to recognise how these – for obvious electoral and political reasons – were sectional interests: 'it would not be right for me to look at this matter in any other way than as the leader of a great national party. I am trying to handle these matters with the best judgment but in the spirit of the whole country'.[21] Congress was dominated by southern interests, and opposition to the appointment of Black Americans to executive positions was forceful. Wilson's administration reflected this southern dominance. Unsurprisingly, the NAACP took a different view judging segregation enormously damaging to Black employees' career prospects:

> [the NAACP] realizes that this new and radical departure has been recommended, and is now being defended, on the ground that by giving certain bureaus or sections wholly to colored employees they are thereby rendered safer in possession of their offices and are less likely to be ousted or discriminated against. We believe this reasoning to be fallacious. It is based on a failure to appreciate the deeper significance of the new policy; to understand how farreaching the effects of such a drawing of caste lines by the Federal Government may be, and how humiliating it is to the men thus stigmatized.[22]

These objections proved prescient and well-founded. Similar objections were marshalled by the Black activist, Robert Wood: 'intelligence and efficiency cannot now be measured according to the color of skin ... the present system of segregation is surely tending toward the total elimination of colored people from honest employment in the Civil Service of the United States'.[23] Responding to NAACP protests, Wilson again cited 'national considerations' but in a rather less subtle form:

> It would be hard to make any one understand the delicacy and difficulty of the situation I find existing here with regard to colored

people ... I find myself absolutely blocked by the sentiment of Senators; not alone Senators from the South, by any means, but Senators from various parts of the country. I want to handle the matter with the greatest possible patience and tact, and am not without hope that I may succeed in certain directions.[24]

Wilson, of course, was a product of his times: doctrines of white supremacy were prevalent and race relations were premised on the inferiority of Black Americans. Wilson was also anxious to advance the interests of the Democratic Party fresh from its electoral victory in 1912, itself a result of divisions between the Republicans. Thus Wilson may simply have shared the dominant racial attitudes of his era which, combined with clear political aims, resulted in actions patently detrimental to the interests and position of Black American citizens. The language in his correspondence suggests, however, a personal belief in the desirability of routine segregation not much less deep than that held by southern Democrats.

In 1916 Woodrow Wilson successfully campaigned for re-election to the White House, and although he received the endorsement of some prominent Black leaders, dissatisfaction with his failure to appoint Black Americans to senior administrative posts and his tolerance of segregation in the Federal departments alienated many Black voters. In point of fact, Wilson's actions signalled the exclusion of Black Americans in general from administrative positions of authority and their degradation to second-class unequal citizenship status within the civil service departments, and not simply an exposure of the limits of the Democratic party. This Democratic administration set the framework for segregation of government employees by race over the ensuing four decades. Wilson's condonement of segregation ensured the continuing inequality of Black Americans' status within the American polity. His agreement to photographs on applicants' forms facilitated segregation and discrimination.

In sum, the introduction and enforcement of segregation in the Federal government departments in Washington nicely epitomizes the politics and legality of this system in the United States. Politically, its initiation reflected the new electoral clout of the southern Democrats in Congress, the White House and executive, and the weakness of defenders of Black Americans' interests. Judicially, segregation exploited the full boundaries of the 'separate but equal' tenet sanctified by the Supreme Court. Finally, segregation in government departments illustrated the American state's acknowledgement of Black Americans' second-class citizenship, and its power to enforce this status.

III. Implementation of Segregated Race Relations from 1913

The segregationist trend was not recorded in official government statistics, of course, but was watched, fearfully, by several interest groups notably the National Association for the Advancement of Colored People. From October 1913, the NAACP undertook periodic reviews and inventories of segregated race relations in the Federal government.[25]

Shortly after Wilson entered the White House newly appointed members of his Cabinet, acting individually, issued orders to segregate their departments and hastened to effect the new system. In April 1913, the Acting Secretary of the Treasury, (J.S. Williams), objected to integrated work arrangements in the Bureau of Engraving and Printing, reprimanding the Bureau's Director. In the Bureau he noticed in the 'sizing department' an incongruity disturbing to his sensibilities: 'young white women and colored women were working together side by side and opposite each other. At one end of the machine would be a young white girl and opposite a colored girl'. Williams explained his concerns: 'I feel sure that this must go against the grain of the white women. Is there any reason why the white women should not have only white women opposite them on the machines? And is there any reason why the white women and colored women should not be to some extent segregated?'[26] These workers were duly segregated.

Four months later, in July 1913, the Auditor of the Treasury Department issued an order, on the authority of newly appointed Secretary William McAdoo (a southerner), designating separate toilets for white and black employees.[27] The Assistant Secretary, Williams, wrote his Chief Clerk on July 12 1913: 'I think it would be best for this Department if you should make arrangements by which white and colored employees of this Department shall use different toilet rooms. Please arrange accordingly'.[28] Whether this instruction constituted a formal directive or order was much disputed. The Bureau's own Director denied that an order existed in a letter to a congressman enquiring about the segregationist practice:

> ... I am unable to furnish you with the copy requested as there has been no such formal order issued, but I would add that for a great many years past separate dressing-rooms and wash-rooms have always been provided for the colored employes in this Bureau and recently, in conformity with this custom and because it is a more satisfactory arrangement, separate toilets were assigned for the exclusive use of the colored employees.[29]

None the less, the directive clearly set the tone for a shift to segregated race relations.

In a strategy exploited for the next 50 years, the consent of Black

American employees in these arrangements was cited by Mr Ralph: 'colored employes have expressed themselves as believing that arrangements of this kind, including separate toilet facilities, were very satisfactory and proper, and it would seem that the claim of discrimination is made only by colored persons who do not desire to associate with members of their own race'.[30] Such a view must have pleased the Treasury Secretary McAdoo[31] and indeed President Wilson. The same employees colluded in separate dining arrangements:

> a number of colored assistants preferred to keep together at lunch-time and eat their luncheons in the dressing rooms instead of at the tables in the lunch-room and to accommodate these girls, stools and tables were provided in an enclosed portion of the dressing room very near the lunch-room and this arrangement has proven very acceptable and satisfactory to those that take advantage of it.[32]

In another memorandum, the Bureau's Director's logic deserted him and he resorted to assertion: 'in the lunchroom used by the printers' assistants, many of whom are colored, and where there are six tables, two of the tables were assigned especially for the use of the colored girls for the reason that it is believed that it would be better for them to associate together when eating their luncheons'.[33] Bureau Director Ralph hastened to replace a Black supervisor with a white one in the Wetting Division, in response to a complaint.[34]

In response to the segregation policy, the secretary of the National Independent Political League protested to Wilson: 'if separate toilets are provided for Latin, Teutonic ... Slavic, Semitic and Celtic Americans, then and then only would African Americans be assigned to separation without insult and indignity'.[35] In common with the NAACP, the League was an indefatigable opponent of segregation. Its Secretary, William Monroe Trotter, had several meetings with Wilson. Trotter emphasized the strong association of these practices with Wilson's administration: 'the inauguration of this policy..can be attributed to no cause but the personal prejudice of your appointees in the Executive Branch of the Government. Never before was race prejudice and race distinction made official under our National Government, never before incorporated in a National Government policy'.[36]

A year later Director Ralph was still facetiously enforcing the codes of segregation. This time his alarm was occasioned by the deficiencies of the Treasury's new building: 'the necessity for separate toilet and dressing rooms was overlooked and there is a shortage of toilets in the building due to a lack of funds'. Ever the resourceful pragmatist, he accepted that it would be 'difficult to at once make any arrangements for the separation of the colored employes in these rooms' but promised to do so speedily: 'after we have been located in the new building a month or so, it will be possible for me to devise some means of making proper arrangements'. However, this arrangement necessitated permitting, in the short term, the dreaded 'commingling of the two races in the work and other rooms. I believe that I will be able to settle the matter eventually without difficulty, but deem it my duty to call your attention to this condition in case there may be any discussion of it'.[37] Curiously, 'commingling' could be tolerated as a temporary arrangement but was unthinkable for permanent organization.

The Diffusion of Segregation[38]

In October 1913 the NAACP conducted a systematic study of segregation in Federal government departments in Washington.[39] Its author discovered that the practice initiated in the Treasury Department had rapidly been emulated in other departments, such as the Post Office,[40] though some (such as Agriculture) had resisted the trend. The NAACP had received complaints about segregation in departments for several months before commissioning its study, as a letter in July from Executive Secretary Villard to President Wilson makes plain: 'the colored people everywhere are greatly stirred up over what they consider the hostile attitude of the Administration in regard to colored employees in the government departments'.[41]

A copy of the NAACP's October report was forwarded to President Wilson by the NAACP.[42] The study examined several departments: the Post Office Department; the Treasury Department including the Office of the Auditor for the Post Office; and the Bureau of Engraving and Printing. Its author, May Nerney, believed that the Wilson administration and the strengthened congressional position of the Democratic party had 'given segregation a tremendous impetus and ... marked its systematic enforcement'.[43] In the Bureau of Engraving and Printing, Nerney learned that 'colored clerks are segregated in work by being placed at separate tables and in separate sections of rooms whenever possible. White guides told the investigator that it was to be the future policy of the Bureau to segregate all its colored employees'.[44] Furthermore, 'colored girls no longer use the lunch rooms which for nine years they have been using in common with white girls'.[45] A similar eviction from dining rooms befell Black workers in the Post Office Department: 'no lunch room is provided for the colored employees in the Post Office Department. The white employees have a very attractive room. The guide advanced as a convincing argument in explanation of this condition that as no restaurants in Washington were open to colored people, the government could not be expected to furnish one'.[46] Of course, it was Congress which was responsible for facilities in Washington. Segregation was occasionally subverted by pragmatism, as Nerney illustrated:

... economic efficiency refuses to follow the color line ... [A] young colored man.. is the only colored clerk employed in a room of white clerks doing the same work. Mr Kram, when asked why he left him here, said he could not spare him as he was his most expert operator. It is trite to point out that here again the colored man is competing not with his own race but with the white man. Segregate the colored man and he will lose this opportunity to develop by competition.[47]

Whether or not 'trite' this observation proved percipient. It illustrates powerfully what occurred in practice: Black Americans were not promoted to supervisory positions unless within segregated units. Nerney argued that, fearful of losing their jobs, Black employees were reluctant to protest the new arrangements.[48] The diffusion of segregation was underpinned by subtle justification, consistent with prevailing societal values. This NAACP prepared report is a seminal document in the history of segregation in federal government departments.

The segregation of the civil service was assisted, without doubt, by the sentiments of many residents in Washington who themselves appeared, to many observers, largely indistinguishable from southerners. Thus one correspondent of the NAACP believed that the new practices were 'done on the initiative of subordinate chiefs who would like to have done it long ago but dared not, or who, mostly newly-appointed Southerners, took the first opportunity'.[49] These subordinate chiefs received no discouragement from their superiors, and the chief executive himself concurred in the new policy. At the Treasury Department, Secretary William McAdoo refused to accept that the measures he supported constituted segregation. McAdoo then described practices, which to most observers would be adjudged segregation: 'negroes have been put at separate desks in the same room with whites, and there has been no discrimination against them in the matter of light, heat, air, furniture or treatment'.[50] He does not reveal who made the complaints about integration. Thirteen months later the Treasury Secretary was still embattled in correspondence defending practices under his authorization. He wrote the editor of *World* that:

> the charge is *untrue* as to the Treasury Department except to this extent: *separate toilets* have been assigned to whites and blacks in the Treasury building and in the office of the Auditor of the Interior Department. The toilets assigned to the blacks are just as good as those assigned to the whites. There is no discrimination in quality. I do not know that this can properly be called segregation.[51]

If this was not segregation it is difficult to imagine what arrangement would have earned the sobriquet. McAdoo formulated a tortuous justification for this separation of ablutions facilities based wholly on the prejudice of white employees: 'it is difficult to disregard certain feelings and sentiments of white people in a matter of this sort. The whites constitute the great majority of the employees and are entitled to just consideration'. He also claimed that segregation by race was no different than hierarchical differentiation: 'any more, for instance, than the provision of separate toilets for the higher officials of the department would be a denial of the rights of the ordinary employees'.[52] Unfortunately this was exactly wrong: the pretence of 'separate but equal' facilities was not that it did not rest upon hierarchy but offered the same arrangements to the segregated group.

The concerns of Black activists were stirred over a different aspect of Black employment in the Federal government in May 1914, when the US Civil Service Commission made photographs a mandatory component on all application forms.[53] This requirement – superseded only in 1940 with an impartial fingerprint – concerned Black Americans for several decades, and was an obvious instrument of discrimination in the appointment of applicants.[54] The NAACP complained to President Wilson in 1915 that the Commission had conceded that photographs were used for several purposes:

> in correspondence with our attorney, officers of the United States Civil Service Commission have admitted that these photographs are not to be used solely for purposes of identification to prevent impersonation at examination but, it is acknowledged, they are also to be available to the appointing officer to assist him in making his choice from among the candidates certified by the Commission as successful.[55]

The shift to photographs strengthened Black groups' criticisms of the Democratic administration and, although it is unknown 'whether or not this change was directed solely at Negro applicants for public office',[56] given the political context and the existing concerns about segregation its association to the latter policy can hardly have been unrecognized by the Commission. The requirement complemented the policy of segregation under way in departments such as the Post Office and Treasury. Writing a decade later, the president of Howard University described the damage caused by requiring a photograph from applicants:

> when Theodore Roosevelt, that superlative American, was Civil Service Commissioner, under the administration of Grover Cleveland, he insisted that every applicant should have a square deal, and especially that there should be no discrimination on account of race or color. Many competent colored men and women entered the Service

in those days, and have served the government with satisfaction. But at the present time the applicant is required to submit a photograph, and is left at the mercy of the head of the bureau to which he is certified ... What warrant has the Civil Service Commission for presuming to judge the mind's construction in the fact? The essential principle of democracy is violated by such presumption. Nor can it be claimed that the photograph is necessary for identification of the applicant. The only practical purpose served is to exclude the applicant whose face shows pigmentation. The option of the head of the bureau to select from several submitted names works to the same end where he has foreknowledge of the race identity of the contestants.[57]

The same writer urged replacing photographs with fingerprints. A 1928 survey of segregation in government departments by the NAACP found that some 'Department Heads frankly admitted that the photograph required by the Civil Service Commission is of value in eliminating Negro eligibles after certification by the Civil Service Commission'.[58]

These measures reduced the number of Black Americans working in the Federal civil service. According to one source the percentage of Black employees fell from six per cent in 1910 to 4.9 per cent in 1918.[59] Writing in 1958, Van Riper argued that the 'period from 1913 to 1921 deserves to be considered the most critical period in the recent history of Negro federal civil employment. Historically, the Negroes have received their greatest inducement to enter the public service under Republican administrations'.[60] This is, in my view, something of an understatement which fails to acknowledge the setbacks to the position of Black Americans in relation to the Federal government and the legacies of these setbacks.

William Monroe Trotter, secretary of the National Independent Political League and editor of the Boston *Guardian*, had several meetings with President Wilson to protest segregation in the civil service. Wilson soon tired of Trotter, accusing him of unacceptable rudeness. In November 1913, Trotter met with the President to submit a petition signed by 20,000 persons seeking a presidential inquiry into segregation in the Federal government. He maintained that segregation necessarily implied inequality for Black employees: ' ... this is true of segregation at desks or in rooms, already notorious under the auditors of the Post Office, the Navy, in the Post Office Department, the Bureau of Engraving and elsewhere. This is segregation of African-American employees at the behest of the prejudice of all other racial classes of employees'.[61] Trotter urged the President to end such practices. In his reply, Wilson denied any significant change to policy under his Administration.[62] A year later Trotter returned to visit the President, with a similar agenda: 'we have come back having found that all the forms of segregation of government employees of African extraction are still practiced in the treasury and postoffice department buildings, and ... have spread into other government buildings'.[63]

In defending segregation, Wilson fell back on the claim that his policies would advance Black employees' interests:

> in my view the best way to help the Negro in America is to help him with his independence... I have discussed it with my colleagues in the departments... [And] the point that was put to me, in essence, was that they were seeking, not to put the Negro employees at a disadvantage, but they were seeking to make arrangements which would prevent any kind of friction between the white employees and the Negro employees.[64]

Questioned by Trotter about the effects of segregation, Wilson pleaded that Black Americans view this arrangement differently: 'if you take it as a humiliation, which it is not intended as, and sow the seeds of that impression all over the country, why the consequences will be very serious. But if you should take it in the spirit in which I have presented it to you, it wouldn't have serious consequences'.[65] Trotter's reply was dignified:

> we are not here as wards. We are not here as dependents. We are not here looking for charity or help. We are here as full-fledged American citizens, vouchsafed equality of citizenship by the federal Constitution. Separation and distinction marking, because of a certain kind of blood in our veins, when it is not made against other different races, is something that must be a humiliation. It creates in the minds of others that there is something the matter with us – that we are not their equals, that we are not their brothers, that we are so different that we cannot work at a desk beside them, that we cannot eat at a table beside them, that we cannot go into the dressing-room where they go, that we cannot use a locker beside them, that we cannot even go into a public toilet with them.[66]

Trotter's description of the character, consequences and purpose of segregation applied to the next half-century: 'now, Mr President, there cannot be any friction with regard to going into a public toilet. They have been going into the public toilet for fifty years. They were going into the public toilets when your administration came in. When your administration came in ... a drastic segregation was put into effect almost at once'.[67]

In retrospect, it is clear that Wilson's presidency marked the most significant period for the introduction and dissemination of segregated race relations in the Federal civil service. His appointment of several southern Cabinet Secretaries and agreement to photographs on civil service application forms ensured the persistence of segregation in the 1920s and 1930s. The NAACP was vigilant in analysing its presence and diffusion.[68] In 1925 the NAACP appointed a journalist to establish the scale of segregation. The journalist was directed by Professor Kelly Miller of Howard University, whom the NAACP Secretary urged to 'keep absolutely secret the fact that we have an investigator on the job until we have secured all the information that is necessary or that can possibly be secured'.[69]

In 1927, 36 black employees in the Department of the Interior wrote to the Secretary, Hubert Work, protesting a 'reorganisation' which happened to result in segregation:

> the reorganization recently instituted in the Pension Bureau has, it is believed, by the undersigned meant segregation in its most insidious form ... We have not in the past objected to being transferred and detailed to other divisions, but when almost every colored clerk is put in one division we feel that we have every right to complain. This division which has been created for colored employees exclusively, all white clerks having been removed, is known as the 'Files Division' and the allocation in it are among the lowest in the office.[70]

Moorfield Storey called on President Coolidge to 'carry out' his expressions of support for Black Americans.[71] The NAACP wrote directly to President Coolidge about segregation – 'a situation in the Government Departments in Washington which is deeply stirring the sentiment of colored citizens throughout the United States'. The letter continued: 'colored people feel that under your administration they have a right to expect that such practices, expressive of the Jim Crow spirit and a relic of slavery days, will receive the rebuke which they deserve'.[72] However, the Republican administrations of the 1920s were uninterested in addressing these issues by now closer to the Democratic Party on segregation.

The NAACP's 1928 survey of segregation was based on visits to each department and interviews with both departmental heads and clerks.[73] One general finding was a gender distinction: 'Negro women seem to suffer more from race discrimination than do the men. Negro employees graded as laborers and messengers are not confronted with race distinction as a general rule'. There was a relatively uncomplicated explanation for this pattern: 'this may be due largely to the fact that most laborers and messengers are Negroes'.[74]

Statistical data about Black American employment in the US federal government, collected in 1928, alarmed the NAACP.[75] These data provided a profile of the distribution of Black employees across departments. The

NAACP's Assistant Secretary, Walter White, was concerned about both the appointment of Black applicants to positions in the Federal government and their subsequent promotion.[76] He later formulated a four point strategy for ascertaining data about these phenomena, including writing to appointing officers and to leading Black Americans in Washington, and interviewing the Civil Service Commission.[77] For many departments and bureaux it was on occasion impossible to obtain reliable information. In some instances, no segregation was unearthed. Some departments solved the problem by hiring Black employees for custodial positions only, such as State.[78]

Furthermore, how senior government administrators and Cabinet members assessed the presence or absence of segregation did not always coincide with the judgements of outsiders. Thus, the Secretary of the Treasury in 1928, Andrew Mellon, rejected the term segregation on the grounds that, 'in every branch of the Department the colored employees are intermingled with white employees'. Any segregation observed was for a different reason according to Mellon:

> in the Register's Office the colored and white employees are working together in the same room. In the Treasurer's Office there is no grouping of employees by reason of color although it happens that the separation of certain colored men and white women employees in separate rooms has resulted in placing the five colored employees in a separate room, but it will be obvious to you that this separation on the basis of sex is more pleasant for both groups and this was the reason for the separation.[79]

In further correspondence with Secretary Mellon, reporting the incidence of segregation after a visit, the NAACP tried to explain to him why such demarcation was objectionable:

> many whites cannot understand why Negroes object to segregation in their work, and regard such matters as complaints about separate locker rooms and segregated parts of lunchrooms as trivial ... It is obvious that a worker whom a caste prescription segregates has very little opportunity for advancement, and a segregated locker room loses its insignificance when it becomes a symbol of the belief that the Negro is unfit to associate with his fellow workers of the other race.[80]

In sum, segregated race relations arrived decisively in the Federal government in the years following the election of Woodrow Wilson to the White House and the concurrent success of the Democrats in the Congress. Their introduction proved durable and they set the pattern for Black American experience of the Federal government until the 1960s.

IV. The Maintenance of the Segregated State 1913–32

Why did the defeat of the Democrats in 1920 and the return of Republican majorities to the Congress and the election of Republican presidents (Warren Harding 1921–23, Calvin Coolidge 1923–29 and Herbert Hoover 1929–33) not end segregated race relations in the Federal government? There are several factors.

First, the migration of tens of thousands of southern Black Americans to northeastern and Midwestern cities during and after the First World War stimulated massive racism and conflict and Republicans did not wish to alienate white supporters. The Ku Klux Klan enjoyed a marked revival in the 1920s and racial tension in eastern and Midwestern cities was intense. Spurred on by Griffiths' virulently racist film, *Birth of a Nation* (which the NAACP tried to get banned[81]), the so-called second Klan of the 1920s recruited strongly during this decade.[82]

Second, and partly as a consequence of the first factor, the Republican party was apprehensive about publicly appealing to Black American voters. This distancing was rooted in a process beginning at the turn of the century as the Republicans gradually accepted the Jim Crow practices spreading throughout the South, and absorbed commonplace criticisms of Black American politicians' inadequacies in the Reconstructed Southern states. Republicans were the majority party after 1877, making this shift in their position toward Black Americans important. It was not incongruous with the Party's antebellum views. C. Vann Woodward imputes a significant ambivalence to the Party's attitude at the end of the Civil War, 'on the issue of Negro equality the party remained divided, hesitant, and unsure of its purpose'. Consequently, the 'historic commitment to equality it eventually made was lacking in clarity, ambivalent in purpose, and capable of numerous interpretations'.[83] This ambivalence was not eradicated by the persistence in the North of racist attitudes and, in some cases, segregated practices. The Republican commitment to Black Americans' interests continued to fade in the new century. V.O. Key documents the progressive, Theodore Roosevelt's (1901–9), role in shifting the Republicans towards a more hostile position about race relations, pushing the Party in the 'same direction that the Democrats had been moving, only not so far'.[84]

By the first decade of this century, Republicans weakly defended the right of Black Americans to vote. George Frederickson traces this change in the Progressive Theodore Roosevelt: 'earlier in his Presidency he had talked and acted as if he had some concern with maintaining the rights of Negroes to citizenship and political participation, but by 1905 he had obviously decided that the best approach was one which relied on the paternalisitic mercies of the "better class" of Southern whites'.[85] Democratic control of the presidency was rare between 1877 and 1932, and the Republicans also dominated Congress in the fifteen years before 1913. Consequently, the neglect of Black Americans' interests by Republicans was significant, and indeed Theodore Roosevelt 'reduced the number of Negro officeholders'.[86] By the 1920s and the Harding-Coolidge presidencies, Republicans were disinclined to woo Black American voters, whose vote they were accustomed to receiving as the Party of Lincoln.[87]

In Congress, Republicans distanced themselves from the concerns of Black American voters, although they rarely articulated racist or segregationist policy. The Republican presidents succeeding Woodrow Wilson paid lip-service to the need for civil rights and blamed Democrats for their absence. Neither Warren Harding (1921–23) nor the conservative Calvin Coolidge (1923–29) actively encouraged segregation but both failed to respond to requests from Black interest groups to desegregate, and disregarded the mobilization of the Ku Klux Klan in the 1920s. An increase in white racism accompanied the large-scale migration of southern Blacks – close to a million in the whole decade[88] – to the North. Republicans hoped to retain the traditional loyalties of the Black American electorate but were unwilling to appeal to them directly for fear of alienating white northern voters. This migration fostered both racist attitudes and sharper residential segregation. With the brief exception of Herbert Hoover (1929–33) – perhaps anticipating the electoral seachange of 1932 – who attempted to appeal more directly to Black voters in 1928 by desegregating one section of the Commerce Department, Republicans were unsympathetic to Black voters' needs.

Third, Democratic members of Congress were quick to rebuke departmental officials for desegregating. Thus the abolition of segregation in the Census Bureau of the Department of Commerce in 1928 by the then Secretary, Herbert Hoover,[89] was immediately criticized by Senators Cole Blease of South Carolina, Hubert Stephens of Mississippi and Thomas Heflin of Alabama in Congress. Blease inserted critical newspaper articles in the *Congressional Record* and excoriated Hoover and his presidential ambitions. In tasteless prose, Blease assured his colleagues that Hoover would never 'break the solid South by putting 'chocolate drops' in the same water-closet with young white girls'.[90] Senator Stephens asserted that, 'there has been no demand for this change except that coming from negro politicians outside the service'.[91] Senator Blease told the Senate:

> in the South we believe that white supremacy is a part of the Christian religion, that the white people are superior to negroes, and we never expect under any conditions or circumstances to permit social equality in that section of the country … and if such a policy as has been

started by Mr Herbert Hoover is to be put in operation, those who
have been sleeping in their beds at night and waking up in the morning
with the happy thought that the South will ever have a respectable
Republican Party had just as well go back to bed and stay there,
because no such condition will ever arise.[92]

Senator Thomas Heflin from Alabama concurred with Blease's attack on
desegregation:

> what right has he [Hoover] to disturb the splendid segregation
> arrangements established in the Commerce Department by the
> Democratic Party, under which the negroes were working and getting
> along well in one section and the whites were working in another and
> pleased with the situation? They tell us that the high-brow negro
> organization for the advancement of the colored race called on Mr
> Hoover and demanded that he do just what he has done in his 'social
> equality' move in the Commerce Department. So Mr Hoover comes
> now, in his effort to get delegates to a Republican National
> Convention, and is putting negro men and women in the offices to
> work alongside white women and girls. He has broken up the
> segregation plan that we had, and now he is distributing negroes all
> through the department promiscuously by placing them alongside of
> whites.[93]

A week later Senator Cole Blease re-entered the fray charging Hoover's
supporters with effecting desegregation in the Interior and Treasury
departments to win Black voters: Hoover had devised a 'systematic plan to
humiliate white girls from whatever part of this Nation they may happen to
come by placing some of them in the same category with negro employees
not only in the offices but in closets in the various departments'.[94]

Thus, any Republicans mindful to address segregation in the Federal
government faced considerable impediments. Within American society,
racial tension and increasing Black American populations outside the South
were disincentives to promulgating strong appeals. In the Federal
government scrutiny from Congress by Democrats – despite the Republican
majority – made desegregation a costly and unattractive strategy.

V. Conclusion

Scholars need to revise theories of American political development and of
the American state to take account of the racial dimension articulated above.
The need for revision takes several forms.

First, enthusiasts for 'bringing the state back in' have correctly drawn attention to the importance of the 'state' as an independent variable in the study of American politics.[95] But these scholars have failed to explain how distinctive the racial dimension of the American state was after 1913. The legacy of this 'peculiar institution' for the relationship between Black Americans and the Federal government is elemental.

Second, the entrenchment of segregation in the Federal government could not but define in part the character of the American state, as Robert Wood explained in a letter to President Wilson:

> ... as American citizens sincerely interested in the welfare of the country as a whole, we resent the segregation and the discrimination in the Federal Civil Service because, however necessary and important the enforced segregation of the races may be to the voters in rural communities in Alabama or Mississippi and to their candidates for office, it is not a business in which this great nation can engage with any profit to the people as a whole, and it can be productive only of evil and ill will among a large and important minority.[96]

To view this state as 'weak' and 'inconsequential', the conventional scholarly perspective, is embarrassingly to omit the experience of Black Americans. This point was expressed forcefully by the labour organizer, A Philip Randolph, who remarked in 1943 that Black Americans occupied 'a position different from that of any other section of the population of this country'. Black Americans found themselves compelled to struggle against the state: 'The Negroes are in the position of having to fight their own Government ... because the Government today is the primary factor, the major factor, in this country in propagating discrimination against Negroes. It is perpetuating and freezing an inferior status of second-class citizenship for Negroes in America'.[97] In the decades before the Civil Rights Act of 1964, the Federal government used its power to impose a pattern of segregated race relations among its employees and, through its programmes (such as housing and employment services), upon the whole of American society well beyond the Mason-Dixon line. This pattern structured the relationship between ordinary Black Americans and the US Federal government – whether as employees in government agencies, inmates or officers in federal prisons, inductees in the Armed Services, consumers of federally guaranteed mortgages or jobseekers in United States Employment Service offices or visitors to National Parks in which the facilities were segregated.

Third, the Federal government's endorsement and, on occasions, implementation of the segregated race relations provided a litmus test for society. Americans outside the state could point to the behaviour of the

Federal government to justify their own segregationist arrangements. This inference was drawn by one correspondent of the NAACP in 1924 who observed: 'while ... segregation exists in the departments in Washington, the United States sets an example which justifies the Ku Klux Klan and every other effort to keep the colored people down'.[98] Segregated race relations imposed second-class status upon Black American employees. It was not until the outbreak of the Second World War that this consequence was acknowledged within the Government. A wartime confidential study, entitled 'Negroes in a Democracy at War', recognized the harm of Black Americans' exclusion from government: 'in the fact that the Government itself fails to employ Negroes in jobs for which they are qualified lies a pretext which private industry utilizes for its persistent discrimination against the colored race'.[99]

The US state created in the post-1913 years was unequivocally a segregated one and without acknowledgement of this dimension scholarly accounts of the American state will be deficient and inadequate.

NOTES

1. The research upon which this study is based is used more extensively in my book *Separate and Unequal: Black Americans and the US Federal Government* (Oxford and New York: Oxford University Press, 1995) to which the reader is directed for additional information.
2. E. Foner, *Reconstruction: American's Unfinished revolution 1863–1877* (New York: Harper & Row), 1988, p.603.
3. For earlier studies see A. Meier and E. Rudwick 'The Rise of Segregation in the Federal Bureaucracy 1900–1930', *Phylon*, Vol.28 (1967), pp.178–84, S Krislou *The Negro in Federal Employment: The Quest for Equal Opportunity* (Minneapolis, MN: University of Minnesota Press, 1967) and N.J. Weiss, 'The Negro and the New Freedom: Fighting Wilsonian Segregation', *Political Science Quarterly, Vol.*LXXXIV, (1969), pp.61–79.
4. On the diversity of the American political tradition see L. Hartz in *The Liberal Tradition in America* (New York: Harcourt, Brace & World, 1955), J.D. Greenstone, *The Lincoln Persuasion,* (Princeton, NJ: Princeton University Press, 1993), and R.M. Smith in 'Beyond Tocqueville, Myrdal, and Hartz: The Multiple Traditions in America', *American Political Science Review,* Vol.87, (1993), pp.549–66.
5. *Papers of Woodrow Wilson,* Vol.28, (Princeton NJ: Princeton University Press, 1978), letter to WW from Moorfield Storey [NAACP President] and Others, 15 Aug. 1913, p.165.
6. Prior to the end of segregation, the United States was sub-nationally a divided polity, reflecting the sectional division between the North and the South. Two political systems, mirroring two societies, the one democratic and the other oligarchic, existed side by side. This sectionalism defined almost every other aspect of the political system including presidential elections, congressional politics and the powers and limits of the Federal government. See R.F. Bensel, *Sectionalism and American Political Development 1880–1980* (Madison, WI: University of Wisconsin Press, 1982), V.O. Key, *Southern Politics,* (New York: Knopf, 1949), J.M. Kousser *The Shaping of Southern Politics: Suffrage Rrestriction and the Establishment of the One-Party South, 1880–1910,* (New Haven, CT: Yale University Press, 1974), and J.M. Kousser, 'The Voting Rights Act and the Two Reconstructions' in B. Grofman and C. Davidson (eds.), *Controversies in Minority Voting,* (Washington, DC: Brookings Institution, 1992). See also D. Rueschmeyer, E. Stephens and J. Stephens,*Democracy and Capitalist Development,* (Chicago: University of Chicago Press, 1992).

7. See the section on 'Benefit to the Colored Race' in US Civil Service Commission *Eighth Report of the US Civil Service Comission July 1 1890 to June 30 1891* (Washington, DC: Government Printing Office, 1891), p.6.
8. In 1893 the US Civil Service Commission's annual report included an initial inventory of Black employees in the Federal service listed below:

Black Employment in the Federal Government, 1893

Agency	Number
Executive Mansion:	5
Public Buildings and Grounds:	
the Commissioner employs	53
Department of State:	
consuls:	4
messengers:	5
laborers	7
Treasury Department:	
Total (excluding below)	168
Bureau of Engaving and Printing	146
Coast Survey	17
Collectors of custom	3
Interior Department:	354
Recorder of Deeds in DC (Hon Blanche Bruce)	
War Department:	174
Navy Department:	8
Post Office Department:	70
Mail-bag repair	42
Department of Agriculture:	37
Smithsonian Institute:	29
Public Printing Office:	
The Public Printer	204
United States Senate:	36
House of Representatives:	
Capitol police and architect's office	27
Librarian of the House	1
Library of Congress:	4
Commissioners of the District:	
Laborers, clerks, teachers, superintendents assessors etc	1000
Office of Recorder of deeds, DC:	
permanent	14
temporary	5
Washington City post-office:	68
Total in executive departments and other branches of Government	2,393

Source: US Civil Service Commission *Ninth Report of the US Civil Service Commission July 1 1891 to June 30 1892* (Washington, DC: Government Printing Office 1893), pp.236-7.

9. P.P. Van Riper, *History of the United States Civil Service* (Evanston, IL: Row, Peterson & Co., 1958),. p.162.
10. See entries under 'District of Columbia' and 'Colored People' in the Congressional Record 63d Congress, First and Second Sessions; US Congress House of Representatives Committee on Reform in the Civil Service, *Segregation of Clerks and Employees in the Civil Service,*

86 DEMOCRACY AND NORTH AMERICA

Hearings, 63d Congress, 2nd Session, 1914. In the First Session HR 5968, and in the Second Session HR 13772 and HR 17541 each proposed segregation by race in the civil service. On DC see Hearing before the Committee on the District of Columbia, 64d Congress 1st Session on HR 12, HR 13, HR 274, HR 326, HR 618, HR 715, and HR 748, 11 Feb. 1916, 'Intermarriage of Whites and Negroes in the District of Columbia and Separate Accommodations in Street Cars for Whites and Negroes in the District of Columbia', 30 pp.
On the civil service see also National Archives, Record Group 233, Records of the U.S. House of Representatives, 63d Congress, Committee on the Civil Service, Box 484, and M. Sasna, 'The South in the Saddle: Racial Politics During the Wilson Years', *Wisconsin Magazine of History*, Vol.LIV (1970).

11. *Congressional Record*, 63d Congress, Second Session, Vol.55, Part 2, 27 June, p.11278, HR 17541 introduced by Senator Park to the Committee on Military Affairs.
12. *Congressional Record*, 63d Congress, 1st Session, Vol.50, Part 2, 10 June 1913, p.1985. Assigned to the Committee on Reform in the Civil Service.
13. 'Intermarriage of Whites and Negroes in the District of Columbia' and 'Separate Accommodations in Street Cars for Whites and Negroes in the District of Columbia', Hearings before the Committee on the District of Columbia, House of Representatives, Sixty-fourth Congress, First Session on HR 12, HR 13, HR 274, HR 326, HR 618, HR 715 and HR 748, 11 Feb. 1916.
14. .Library of Congress Manuscript Division, Papers of the NAACP Group I Box C403, File: Segregation – 27–31 Aug. 1913. Letter from Senator Theodore E. Burton, 10 Sept. 1913 to Frank Morgan in Cleveland Ohio. Opponents of segregation in the Federal government generally lacked a majority: Library of Congress Manuscript Division, Papers of the NAACP, Group I Box C403, File: Segregation, 27–31 Aug. 1913. See letters to the NAACP from Congressman Andrew Peters, 29 Aug. 1913, Senator Theodore E. Burton, 1 Sept. 1913, and Senator Lawrence Y. Sherman, 3 Sept. 1913.
15. *Congressional Record*, 63d Congress, First Session, Senate, Vol.51, Part 12, 8 July, p.11798.
16. *Papers of Woodrow Wilson*, Vol.28, (Princeton, NJ: Princeton University Press, 1978), letter from John Palmer Gavit to Oswald Garrison Villard, 1 Oct. 1913, p.350. The correspondent of the NAACP noted, before 1913, 'the white men and women in the Government service always have resented being compelled to associate with the negroes'. Little was done to accommodate this resentment before the Democratic Party success, however. Gavit also noted that the new practices were 'done on the initiative of subordinate chiefs who would like to have done it long ago but dared not, or who, mostly newly-appointed Southerners, took the first opportunity', ibid., p.350.
17. Although perhaps a less dramatic break in relation to Black Americans than often assumed. By 1912 the NAACP was openly criticizing the Taft adminsitration's failure to advance Black Americans' interests, and in the case of the Post Office, to hinder them. See *The Crisis*, Feb. 1912.
18. K.A. Clements, *The Presidency of Woodrow Wilson* (Lawrence, KS: University Press of Kansas, 1992), p.45.
19. K.A. Clements, *The Presidency of Woodrow Wilson* (Lawrence, KS: University Press of Kansas, 1992), p.45.
20. K.A. Clements, *The Presidency of Woodrow Wilson* (Lawrence, KS: University Press of Kansas, 1992), p.46. See also H. Blumenthal, 'Woodrow Wilson and the Race Question', *Journal of Negro History*, Vol.48 (1963), pp.1–21.
21. *Papers of Woodrow Wilson*, Vol.28, (Princeton, NJ: Princeton Univrsity Press, 1978), letter from WW to Thomas Dixon, Jr., 29 July 1913, p.94.
22. *Papers of Woodrow Wilson*, Vol.28, (Princeton, NJ: Princeton University Press, 1978), letter from NAACP President, Moorfield Storey and others to WW, 15 Aug. 1913, p.165.
23. *Papers of Woodrow Wilson*, Vol.28, (Princeton, NJ: Princeton University Press, 1978), letter from Robert Wood to WW, 5 Aug. 1913, p.117.
24. *Papers of Woodrow Wilson*, Vol.28, (Princeton, NJ: Princeton University Press, 1978), letter to NAACP Secretary Oswald Garrison Villard from WW, 21 Aug. 1913, p.202.
25. For a fuller account of the statistical and documentary sources available to students of Black American employment in the Federal government see D.S. King, *Separate and Unequal:*

Black Americans and the US Federal Government (Oxford and New York: Oxford University Press, 1995).

26. National Archives, Record Group 318 Records of the Bureau of Engraving and Printing, Central Correspondence File, 1913–39, Box 6, File: Segregation, 1913. Memorandum from Mr Williams for Mr Ralph, Director Bureau of Engraving and Printing, 3 April 1913. Ralph replied: 'I could not put in writing many things in regard to the matter referred to by you which it would be well to take up, but will discuss the same with you when you call at this Bureau'.

27. *The Papers of Woodrow Wilson,* Vol.28, (Princeton, NJ: Princeton University Press, 1978), p.491.

28. Library of Congress Manuscript Division, Papers of the NAACP Group, I Box C402, File: Segregation – Federal Service, 12 July–24 Aug. 1915. Copy in this folder.

29. National Archives Record Group 318, Records of the Bureau of Engraving and Printing, Central Correspondence File 1913–39, Box 6, File: Segregation, 1913. Letter from J.E. Ralph, Director to Congressman E.F. Kinkead, 14 Aug. 1913.

30. National Archives Record Group 318, Records of the Bureau of Engraving and Printing, Central Correspondence File 1913–39, Box 6, File: Segregation, 1913. Letter from J.E. Ralph, Director of the Bureau to Secretary of the Treasury, William G. McAdoo, 6 Dec. 1913, pp.2–3.

31. McAdoo was a close contender for the Democratic party presidential nomination in 1924.

32. National Archives Record Group 318, Records of the Bureau of Engraving and Printing, Central Correspondence File 1913–39, Box 6, File: Segregation, 1913. Letter from J.E. Ralph, Director of the Bureau to Secretary of the Treasury, William G. McAdoo, 6 Dec. 1913, p.3.

33. National Archives Record Group 318, Records of the Bureau of Engraving and Printing, Central Correspondence File 1913–39, Box 6, File: Segregation, 1913. Memorandum from J.E. Ralph, Director of the Bureau to Assistant Secretary of the Treasury, Williams, 12 July 1913, pp.3, p,1.

34. Writing to the complainant,

    in reply to your letter ... in which you state that the superintending of work upon the tables is so closely associated with the ladies that it would be less humiliating to have a white man in charge, I beg to thank you for bringing this matter to my attention as it was not known to me that a white man was not in charge of this work, and upon investigation, I find that the chief of the wetting division under the rule of seniority had permitted Louis H Nutt, a negro, to be in charge of the work, who, however was classified as a skilled helper and had not officially been designated as foreman of the work. I wish to state that I have this day placed Irving P. Tade, a white man, in charge of the work in question, and I am sure there will be no further cause for complaint on this account.

    National Archives Record Group 318, Records of the Bureau of Engraving and Printing, Central Correspondence File 1913–39, Box 6, File: Segregation, 1913. Letter from J.E. Ralph, Director of the Bureau to Miss Rose Miller, Wetting Division, 23 July 1913. See also Miller's letter, 19 July 1913. For another instance of white workers objecting to working alongside Black employees see the memorandum of 10 Nov. 1914 to the Bureau Director in RG 318, Records of the Bureau of Engraving and Printing, Central Administrative File 1913–39, Box 6, File: Segregation 1914.

35. *The Papers of Woodrow Wilson,* Vol.28, (Princeton, NJ: Princeton University Press, 1978), letter from William Monroe Trotter to Wilson, 6 Nov. 1913, p.492.

36. *Papers of Woodrow Wilson,* Vol.28, (Princeton, NJ: Princeton University Press, 1978), letter from William Trotter to WW, 6 Nov. 1913, p.493.

37. National Archives Record Group 318, Records of the Bureau of Engraving and Printing, Central Correspondence Files 1913–39, Box 6, File: Segregation 1914. Letter from Bureau Director Ralph to Secretary of the Treasury Hamlin, 7 March 1914.

38. It is worth noting how difficult acquiring data about segregation is. The Federal government, meaning principally the Civil Service Commission, rarely kept data about employees by race (though on occasions it included relevant material in its annual report which I use below) and

nor did the agencies. The scholar is therefore compelled to rely on a range of sources, which, while valuable, are rarely comprehensive.

39. Library of Congress Manuscript Division, Papers of the NAACP, Group I, Box C403, File: Segregation – Federal Service, 27–31 Aug. 1913, contains many letters received during the preparation of the survey.

40. Library of Congress Manuscript Division, Papers of the NAACP, Group I, Box C403 File: Segregation – Federal Service, 12 July–24 Aug. 1913, circular letter from NAACP, 18 Aug. 1913.

41. *Papers of Woodrow Wilson*, Vol .28, (Princeton, NJ: Princeton University Press, 1978), letter to WW from Oswald Garrison Villard, 21 July 1913, p.60. See also the letter from Alfred B. Cosey to Joseph Patrick Tumulty, 22 Aug. 1913, ibid., pp.209–12.

42. *Papers of Woodrow Wilson*, Vol.28, (Princeton, NJ: Princeton University Press, 1978), letter to WW from Oswald Garrison Villard, NAACP President, enclosing a report by May Childs Nerney, NAACP Secretary on segregation in government departments, 14 Oct. 1913 pp.401–10.

43. *Papers of Woodrow Wilson*, Vol.28, (Princeton, NJ: Princeton University Press, 1978), letter to WW from Oswald Garrison Villard, NAACP President, enclosing a report by May Childs Nerney, NAACP Secretary on segregation in government departments, 14 Oct. 1913, p.402.

44. *Papers of Woodrow Wilson*, Vol.28, (Princeton, NJ: Princeton University Press, 1978), letter to WW from Oswald Garrison Villard, NAACP President, enclosing a report by May Childs Nerney, NAACP Secretary on segregation in government departments, 14 Oct. 1913, p.403.

45. *Papers of Woodrow Wilson*, Vol.28 (Princeton, NJ: Princeton University Press, 1978), letter to WW from Oswald Garrison Villard, NAACP President, enclosing a report by May Childs Nerney, NAACP Secretary on segregation in government departments, 14 Oct. 1913, p.403.

46. *Papers of Woodrow Wilson*, Vol.28, (Princeton, NJ: Princeton University Press, 1978), letter to WW from Oswald Garrison Villard, NAACP President, enclosing a report by May Childs Nerney, NAACP Secretary on segregation in government departments,14 Oct. 1913, p.404.

47. *Papers of Woodrow Wilson*, Vol.28, (Princeton, NJ: Princeton University Press, 1978), letter to WW from Oswald Garrison Villard, NAACP President, enclosing a report by May Childs Nerney, NAACP Secretary on segregation in government departments, 14 Oct. 1913, p.407.

48.

the officials in Washington repeatedly call attention to the fact that the colored people have protested against this [Treasury] order but have made no objection to segregation in their work. The reason is, of course, that the colored people ... resent what they feel to be a personal affront; more important is the fact that they cannot protest against segregation in their work *when no official orders have been issued in this regard*. Should they make such complaint they would be merely asked to cite a discriminating order and failing that would probably be told that the changes that had been made had been necessitated by exigencies in work, color having had nothing to do with it. They would be unable to prove their case and might jeopardize their positions because of 'insubordination'.

Papers of Woodrow Wilson, Vol.28, (Princeton, NJ: Princeton University Press, 1978), letter to WW from Oswald Garrison Villard, NAACP President, enclosing a report by May Childs Nerney, NAACP Secretary on segregation in government departments, 14 Oct. 1913, p.409. A not dissimilar response was met by the authors of the 1928 survey of segregation: Library of Congress Manuscript Division, Papers of the NAACP, Group I, Box C403, File: Segregation – Federal Service, 6 March 1928–21 Feb. 1929. 'Segregation in Government Departments' Reports of Investigations made by W.T. Andrews and Walter White NAACP, 1928, p.1.

49. *Papers of Woodrow Wilson*, Vol.28, (Princeton, NJ: Princeton University Press, 1978), letter from John Palmer Gavit to Oswald Garrison Villard, 1 Oct. 1 1913, p.350.

50. *Papers of Woodrow Wilson*, Vol.28, (Princeton, NJ: Princeton University Press, 1978), letter from William Gibbs McAdoo to Oswald Garrison Villard, 27 Oct. 1913, p.453.

51. *Papers of Woodrow Wilson*, Vol.29, (Princeton, NJ: Princeton University Press, 1979), letter from Secretary McAdoo to F.I. Cobb, editor of *World*, 26 Nov. 1914, p.361.

52. *Papers of Woodrow Wilson*, Vol.29, (Princeton, NJ: Princeton University Press, 1979), letter

from Secretary McAdoo to F.I. Cobb, editor of *World*, 26 Nov. 1914, pp.361–2.

53. National Archives Record Group 146, Records of the US Civil Service Commission, Minutes 1886–1929, Box 21, Minutes of the meeting, 27 May 1914, p.228.

54. Library of Congress Manuscript Division, Papers of the NAACP, Group I, Box C272 , File: Discrimination – Employment, Federal Service, see letters to the Commission from Wilson and Waters, lawyers, 27 July 1914. In another letter, 20 Aug. 1914, the same firm noted: 'the reason given by the Commission for the photograph scheme – "namely, to assist in the identification of applicants when they present themselves for examination" – does not appear in any publication issued by the Commission to date'.

55. Library of Congress Manuscript Division, Papers of the NAACP, Group I, Box C272, File: Discrimination – Employment, Federal Service 1913–15. Letter from NAACP Chairman to Wilson, 23 March 1915.

56. P.P. Van Riper, *History of the United States Civil Service* (Evanston, IL: Row, Peterson and Co., 1958, p.241.

57. Library of Congress Manuscript Division, Papers of the NAACP, Group I, Box C273, File: Discrimination – Employment, Federal Service, 1924. Letter from Professor Kelly Miller to Wm Dudley Foulke, President of the Civil Service Reform Association, 18 Sept. 1923.

58. Library of Congress Manuscript Division, Papers of the NAACP, Group I, Box C403, File: Segregation – Federal Service, 6 March 1928–21 Feb. 21 1929. 'Segregation in Government Departments', Reports of Investigations made by W.T. Andrews and Walter White, NAAP, 1928, p.2.

59. Figures from Lawrence J.W. Hayes, *The Negro Federal Government Worker* (Washington, DC: Howard University, 1941), pp.37–58, cited in P.P. Van Riper, *History of the United States Civil Service* (Evanston, IL: Row, Peterson & Co., 1958). p.242.

60. P.P. Van Riper, *History of the United States Civil Service* (Evanston, IL: Row, Peterson & Co., 1958), p.242.

61. *Papers of Woodrow Wilson*, Vol.28, (Princeton, NJ: Princeton University Press, 1978), Trotter's address to WW, 6 Nov. 1913, p.492.

62. *Papers of Woodrow Wilson*, Vol.28, (Princeton, NJ: Princeton University Press, 1978), Wilson's Reply to Trotter's address, 6 Nov. 1913, p.496.

63. *Papers of Woodrow Wilson*, Vol.29, (Princeton, NJ: Princeton University Press, 1979), an Address to the President by William Monroe Trotter, 12 Nov. 1914, p.299.

64. *Papers of Woodrow Wilson*, Vol.29, (Princeton, NJ: Princeton University Press, 1979), Remarks by Wilson and a Dialogue, 12 Nov. 1914, p.302.

65. *Papers of Woodrow Wilson*, Vol.29, (Princeton, NJ: Princeton University Press, 1979), Remarks by Wilson and a Dialogue, 12 Nov. 1914, p.304.

66. *Papers of Woodrow Wilson*, Vol.29, (Princeton, NJ: Princeton University Press, 1979), Remarks by Wilson and a Dialogue, 12 Nov. 1914, pp.304–5.

67. *Papers of Woodrow Wilson*, Vol.29, (Princeton, NJ: Princeton University Press, 1979), Remarks by Wilson and a Dialogue, 12 Nov. 1914, p.305.

68. Library of Congress Manuscript Division, Papers of the NAACP, Group I, Box C273 File: Discrimination – Government, Federal Service 1925, includes 'Memorandum on Segregation of Civil Service Employees' which documents several cases of segregation. See also the correspondence with individual departments about discrimination in NAACP, Group I, Box C403, File: Segregation – Federal Service, June–Sept. 1928. It includes letters to and from the Office of the Postmaster General, the Secretary of the Treasury and the Director of Public Buildings.

69. Library of Congress Manuscript Division, Papers of the NAACP, Group I, Box C273, File: Discrimination – Emploment, Federal Service 1925, letter from NACP Secretary to Miller 10 Jan. 1925.

70. .Library of Congress Manuscript Division, Papers of the NAACP, Group I, Box C403, File: Segregation – Federal Service 1927, Press release by NAACP, 19 Aug. 1927, including the letter.

71. Library of Congress Manuscript Division, Papers of the NAACP, Group I, Box C403, File: Segregation – Federal Service 1927, letter from Storey to Secretary Work, 14 Oct. 1927.

72. Library of Congress Manuscript Division, Papers of the NAACP, Group I, Box C403, File:

Segregation – Federal Service 1927, letter from NAACP to Coolidge, 7 Dec. 1927.

73. Library of Congress Manuscript Division, Papers of the NAACP, Group I, Box C403, File: Segregation – Federal Service, 6 March 1928–21 Feb. 1929. 'Segregation in Government Departments', Reports of Investigations made by W.T, Andrews and Walter White NAACP, 1928, p.19.

74. Library of Congress Manuscript Division, Papers of the NAACP, Group I, Box C403, File: Segregation – Federal Service, 6 March 1928–21 Feb. 1929. 'Segregation in Government Departments', Reports of Investigations made by W.T, Andrews and Walter White NAACP, 1928, p.19, p,1.

Department:	Number	Total Salaries ($)
Alien Property Custodian	16	19,120
American Battle Monuments Commission	1	1,200
Capitol	187	184,040
Chief Coordinator	1	900
Claims Commission (US and Mexico)	2	2,200
Congressional Library	69	65,678
Department of:		
Agriculture	1,086	907,068
Commerce	686	675,629
Interior	459	473,940
Justice	68	104,720
Labor	92	118,702
Navy	5,427	6,537,278
State	76	81,360
Treasury	5,407	6,024,499
War	5,914	5,149,488
District of Columbia government	3,674	5,141,807
Federal Board for Vocational Education	11	12,360
Federal Reserve Board	22	24,232
Federal Trade Commission	7	6,960
General Accounting Office – Treasury	143	183,380
Government Printing Office	934	1,344,524
Inland Waterways Corporation	3	2,520
International Boundary Commission	1	900
Interstate Commerce Commission	15	16,860
National Advisory Committee for Aeronautics	17	7,389
Mixed Claims Commission	2	2,400
National Military Home	181	81,651
Panama Canal Office	23	23,787
Pan American Sanitary Bureau	1	1,470
Personnel Classification Board	2	2,220
Post Office Department	23,390	35,127,433
Public Buildings and Parks	1,189	1,149,865
Smithsonian Institution	161	120,318
US Board of Tax Appeals	9	11,390
US Botanic Garden	7	7,500
US Bureau of Efficiency	3	3,540
US Civil Service Commission	12	14,580
US Employees' Compensation Commission	2	2,760
US Railroad Administration	1	1,020
US Shipping Board	7	7,560
US Shipping Board – Merchant Fleet Corporation	34	34,980
US Soldiers' Home	27	18,480
US Tariff Commission	7	8,460
US Veterans' Bureau	495	762,805
War Finance Corporation	1	1,260
White House, the	10	12,900
Total	51,882	$64,483,133

Source: Library of Congress Manuscript Division, Papers of the NAACP, Group I, Box C403, File: Segregation – Federal Service, 1928. 'Negroes in the US Service at Close of FY Ended, 30 June 1928'. The data were compiled by the Department of Labor on the basis of returns from individual departments and agencies, and issued by Labor.

75. Black Employees in Federal Government 1928
76. Library of Congress Manuscript Divsion, Papers of the NAACP, Group I, Box C403, File: Segregation – Federal Service, 1928. Memorandum from Walter White to the Board of Directors NAACP, 21 Sept. 1928.
77. Library of Congress Manuscript Division, Papers of the NAACP, Group I, Box C403, File: Segregation – Federal Service, 1928. Memorandum from Walter White to the Conference of Executives NAACP,17 Oct. 1928.
78. *Segregation in Washington,* A Report of the National Committee on Segregation in the Nation's Capital (Chicago, Nov. 1948), p.63. For the background to this study, see Library of Congress Manuscript Division, Papers of the NAACP, Group II, Box A386, File: national Committee on Segregation in the Nation's Capital 1942–49, which includes minutes of the meeting at which the study was agreed upon. In particular see the meeting of 23 Oct. 1946 which includes a detailed plan for the Report's remit.
79. Library of Congress Manuscript Division, Papers of the NAACP, Group I, Box C403, File: Segregation – Federal Service, 1928. Letter from Secretary of the Treasury Andrew Mellon to James Johnson Secretary NAACP, 16 May 1928, pp.2–3.
80. Library of Congress Manuscript Division, Papers of the NAACP, Group I, Box C403, File: Segregation – Federal Service, 1928. Letter from NAACP to Secrerary Mellon, 26 Sept. 1928.
81. See *Fighting a Vicious Film: Protest Against 'The Birth of a Nation'* (Boston, MA: Boston Branch of the NAACP, 1915) in Library of Congress Manuscript Division, Papers of Moorfield Storey, Box 13, Folder: 1915. For the background, and racism more generally, see G.M. Frederickson, *The Black Image in the White Mind* (Hanover, NH: Wesleyan University Press, 1971), pp.275–82.
82. See M. MacLean, *Beyond the Mask of Chivalry* (New York: Oxford University Press, 1994).
83. C. Vann Woodward, 'Seeds of Failure in Radical Race Policy', in F.A. Bonadio (ed.), *Political Parties in American History,* Vol.2, 1828–90 (New York: G.P. Putnam's Sons, 1974), p.735.
84. V.O. Key, Jr., *Politics, Parties and Pressure Groups* (New York: Thomas Y. Crowell Co., 1953), 3rd ed. p.189. See also S.M. Scheiner, 'Theodore Roosevelt and the Negro, 1901–1908', *Journal of Negro History,* Vol..XLVII (1962), pp.169–82.
85. G.M. Frederickson, *The Black Image in the White Mind* (Hanover, NH: Wesleyan University Press, 1971), p.299.
86. G.M. Frederickson, *The Black Image in the White Mind* (Hanover, NH: Wesleyan University Press, 1971), p.301.
87. N.J. Weiss, *Farewell to the Party of Lincoln: Black Politics in the Age of FDR* (Princeton, NJ: Princeton University Press, 1983).
88. R. Farley and W.R. Allen, *The Color Line and the Quality of Life in America* (New York: Russell Sage Foundation, 1987).
89. Library of Congress Manuscript Division, Papers of the NAACP, Group I, Box C403, File: Segregation – Federal Service 1928. 'Hoover Ends Segregation in Commerce Department' press release, 6 April 1927. See article 'Hoover Changes Racial Policy in Census Office – Colored Clerks Now in all Departments', *Washington Post,* 31 March 1928.
90. *Congressional Record,* 70th Congress ,1st Session,Vol.LXIX, Part 6, 10 April 1928, p.6150.
91. *Congressional Record,* 70th Congress, 1st Session, Vol.LXIX, Part 10, 29 May 1928, p.10657.
92. Congressional Record, 70th Congress, 1st Session, Vol.LXIX, Part 6, 10 April 1928, p.6149. There are several pages incorporating the Senator's exchanges with the Civil Service Commission.
93. Congressional Record, 70th Congress, 1st Session, Vol.LXIX, Part 6, 10 April, 1928, p.6175.
94. Congressional Record, 70th Congress, 1st Session, Vol.LXIX, Part 6, 16 April, 1928, p.6487. Blease inserted letters from disgruntled employees in the Record. See also remarks by Senator Reed Smoot of Utah pointing out that all the 'villians' identified were Democrats, ibid., Part 7, p.7593.
95. The principal collection is P. Evans, D. Rueschemeyer and T. Skocpol (eds.), *Bringing the State Back In* (New York and Cambridge: Cambridge University Press, 1985). For other key

texts see S. Krasner, *Defending the National Interest* (Princeton, NJ: Princeton University Press, 1978), J.P. Nettl, 'The State as a Conceptual Variable, *World Politics* 1968, pp.559–92, and S. Skowronek, *Building the American State* (New York: Cambridge University Press, 1982).

96. *Papers of Woodrow Wilson*, Vol.28, (Princeton, NJ: Princeton University Press, 1978), letter from Robert Wood to WW, 5 Aug. 1913, p.118.
97. Library of Congress Manuscript Division, National Urban League Papers. I – Administrative Series. Box 16, Folder: Fair Employment Practices Committee 1942–43. Conference on scope and powers of Committee on Fair Employment Practice held with representatives of minority group organisations to discuss the FEPC's remit, 19 Feb. 1943, p.10.
98. Library of Congress Manuscript Division, Papers of the NAACP, Group I, Box C273, File: Discrimination – Employment, Federal Service 1924, Letter to NAACP, New York branch from Moorfield Storey, 2 Dec. 1924, p.1.
99. National Archives Record Group 16 Office of the Secretary of Agriculture, General Correspondence, Negroes 1940–55, Box 3 Folder: Negroes. 'Negroes in a Democracy at War', Survey of Intelligence Materials No.25, Office of Facts and Figures, Bureau of Intelligence , 27 May 1942, p.27.

Democracy and the Reconstitution of Canada

INES C. MOLINARO

This essay analyses the current efforts to reconstitute Canada as a case study of the changing meaning and pressures on democratic governance. Canada's constitutional impasse is organized around three general attributes or functions of constitutions. The study explains why the disputes that have led to the current constitutional impasse are difficult to resolve given the requirements of formal equality and popular consent as understood and practised in Western liberal democracies.

While democracy is embraced increasingly across the world, democratic institutions and practices in the West are criticized more and more for failing to live up to the promise of democracy. Underlying the multiple indictments of liberal democracy is the perception that basic democratic standards – equality, deliberation and participation – are breached in everyday practice. These substantive criticisms strike at the very definition of democratic governance.

There is no consensus on the outer limits of democracy; at a minimum, democracy entails self-government. The rule of the people or popular sovereignty is grounded in the prevailing practice of free and fair elections in which every citizen's vote has an equal weight (formal equality). In large-scale, populous political communities, the people rule indirectly through their elected representatives. However, the growing dissatisfaction with representative institutions and the exclusion of citizens from direct involvement in the making of public policy have played their part in the deepening cynicism and malaise detectable in Western societies today. Reformers have proposed an array of changes to address this situation, many of which would require the introduction of more direct citizen participation in decision-making. Setting aside questions about the feasibility of direct rule under conditions of mass democracy, it is fitting to consider what skills and circumstances promote and sustain sound public deliberation.

The apparent desire to circumvent representative institutions is fed in part by the disenchantment with party politics and a cynicism towards traditional interest group politics.[1] Moreover, the development of a new and more exclusivist form of pluralism where associations or groupings define themselves according to identities that are involuntary and permanent (for instance, gender, race, ethnicity, or sexual preference), poses a serious challenge to conventional understandings of equality and participation. With respect to equality these groups question the liberal assumption of an abstract individualism that recognizes no salient differences between individuals. These groups demand recognition from the larger political community 'because they feel threatened, diminished, oppressed, or because of all the foregoing'.[2] They are not easily accommodated by the practices of bargaining and compromise associated with interest group politics, as they are not principally or exclusively concerned with attaining material benefits or advantages for their members. In contrast to the conventional practices of democractic representation, these groups demand that they are represented by individuals possessing or 'mirroring' the personal traits of their members.

These brief remarks are intended to indicate that the meaning of liberal democratic governance is changing. Some of this change can be explored in light of the current efforts to reconstitute Canada. I will focus on two pillars of liberal democratic theory: equality and consent. The principle of equality is manifested in the understanding that citizens are formally equal under the law. Liberal democratic regimes distinguish between a public and a private sphere and traditionally make good on the promise to protect the sphere of privacy from unnecessary incursion by the state or the majority by upholding substantive protections in the form of individual rights. While fairness would appear to demand that every individual is recognized as formally equal, we are impelled increasingly to rethink not only the distinction between the public and the private but also whether fairness obliges us to recognize the moral claims of distinct communities within nation-states. The prevailing conception of the modern nation-state is that the 'people' are presumed to be fundamentally homogeneous, despite distinctions of class, status and locality. This 'lie' has become increasingly difficult to sustain in light of the growing pressures for recognition of cultural diversity within Western polities. The fact is that we live in societies which contain a wide array of cultural forms or, as Geertz would have it, 'we are living more and more in the midst of an enormous collage' where 'the world is coming at each of its local points to look more like a Kuwaiti bazaar than like an English gentleman's club'.[3] This reality challenges the prevailing assumption that justice requires that citizens must be treated identically.

The securing of consent under normal circumstances takes the form of aggregating individual preferences. Both the process and the substance of political participation suggest that the quality of democractic deliberation is inadequate to meet the growing demands for meaningful participation. The perception that consent has been secured is undoubtedly the single most important basis for the legitimate exercise of power in liberal democratic regimes. The inadequacies of current practices of participation to secure consent are evident in a situation where citizens are required to deliberate on first principles or what is referred to in Canada as 'mega' constitutional politics.[4]

My argument is that Canada's constitutional impasse is difficult to traverse given the requirements of formal equality and popular consent as understood and practised in Western liberal democracies. These practices limit the possibility for meaningful deliberation of the kind of society that can accommodate 'deep diversity'.[5] I order my discussion of Canada's constitutional impasse according to three general attributes or functions of constitutions. While unique in many respects, the contemporary Canadian situation provides a case study of the changing meaning and pressures on liberal democratic governance.

I. Reconstituting Canada

Canada, according to Peter Russell, has been on a steady, if intermittent, 'constitutional odyssey' since at least 1927 when federal and provincial leaders met for the first time to seek agreement on an acceptable formula to amend the constitution. The Canadian constitution of 1867 (known as the British North America Act) established a federal union but contained no amending procedure, rather the practice of making constitutional changes by petitioning the British Parliament was continued. The inability of federal and provincial political elites to reach agreement on amending procedures enabled Canadians to put aside the larger question of sovereignty.

A constitution may function potentially as an instrument of unity, a nation-building device; this has not been the Canadian experience. While the search for an amending formula continued, in the 1960s Québec pursued its own nation-building project which was bound up with profound cultural, political, intellectual and social transformations. The French Canadians changed their referent to Québécois to more faithfully reflect their newly reconstituted identity. The Québec state was perceived increasingly as a lever of collective emancipation, carrying primary responsibility for ensuring the survival and development of the Québécois culture. In this oversimplified account of the changes in post-war Québec, the important point is that all political parties within Québec became convinced of the necessity for greater autonomy for the government of Québec. It has been argued that since 1867 the power of the legislature and government of Québec has been the first line of defence of the rights of the francophone collectivity in Québec .[6]

The post-war changes culminating in the empowerment of the Québec
state was achieved in the first instance by wresting from the Catholic church
(once the competence imputed to the Québec church and the clerical corps
in representing the interests of the collectivity was eroded), control over
education and health within the province. Additionally, the Québec state
sought to expand its capacities to set economic policy and create a network
of public enterprises, and thereby challenge the power of the English
Canadian bourgeoisie based in Montréal and Toronto. State-building in
Québec meant that incursions by the federal government into areas of
provincial jurisdiction through its spending powers were resisted more
forcefully.[7] Thus the unfinished project of repatriating the Canadian
constitution was enmeshed with Québec's demands to renegotiate its status
and powers within the Canadian federation. Further complications and
pressures ensued with the creation of the pro-independence Parti Québécois
in 1968.[8]

Since 1968 there have been five attempts to reform comprehensively the
Canadian constitution and all have failed to resolve the substantial
disagreement among Canadien(nes), Canadians and Kanataians.[9] The ties
that bind have been severely strained by these inconclusive exercises and
the public mood has been at various times anxious and bored, cynical and
fearful. The current federal Liberal government had promised during the
electoral campaign of 1993 to put aside the issue of constitutional reform
and to focus on the economy. This pledge is unlikely to be sustained as
Québec's governing Parti Québécois is committed to holding a referendum
on sovereignty-association in the near future. The majority of political
leaders associated with the most recent proposed constitutional package of
amendments, the Charlottetown Accord (1992), have been voted out of
office. Moreover, the 1993 Canadian and Québec elections returned
political parties that reject on principle constitutional compromise.

Over time the stakes have been raised, the issues and demands have
become more complex and intertwined, and reconciliation appears elusive. It
is easy enough and tempting to paint a bleak and discouraging picture of the
current constitutional impasse, but it would not be the whole truth. There are
formidable obstacles to any settlement that can be imagined. None the less,
it is possible to see in the Canadian stalemate a unique opportunity to put into
practice a viable alternative to the idea that societies cohere to the extent that
a common, homogeneous national culture brings together disparate parts into
a single whole.[10] Perhaps the single most important impediment will remain
the difficulty of learning 'to grasp what we cannot embrace'.[11]

What are the disagreements which have brought Canadians to their current
impasse? In brief, Canadians disagree about how to reconstitute themselves
so that the multiple groups, regions, peoples and individuals within the

territorial boundaries of Canada can fulfill what Aristotle identified as the basic aims of a political community: living, living together and living well. Alongside the challenge posed by the desire and need on the part of the majority francophone population in Québec for recognition as a distinct society within Canada, Canadian federalism is besieged by demands for self-government by Aboriginal peoples, pressure to reform federal institutions from the long neglected Western provinces, and demands from Charter communities (groups who are specifically recognized in the Charter of Rights and Freedoms) that individual rights be protected from communal claims.

As Alan Cairns argues, the Canadian constitutional debate turns on calls for four competing equalities: the equality of citizens; the equality of provinces; the equality of two nations; and the equality of Aboriginal peoples and non-Aboriginal Canadians.[12] The tensions spawned by these demands for equality reveal the difficulty of locating a unifying vision of Canada. Whether the search for a unifying or single vision of Canada is misplaced or not depends on one's understanding of the Canadian political community. Thus, for some Canadians justice and fairness requires that no compromises are made to the principles of the equality of citizens and the equality of provinces.[13]

In this review of how Canadians arrived at the current deadlock, I begin with the substantial reforms achieved through the 1982 Constitution Act. This reconstruction of the constitutional order was marred by the failure to secure the consent of the Québec government and of the elected members of the Québec legislature. Ironically, in light of the subsequent round of constitutional negotiations, one significant reform required amendments to be ratified by provincial legislatures. The new amending formulae are quite complex and for our purposes we need only note that underlying the amending procedures is the principle of the equality of the provinces. No longer requiring approval of the British Parliament, the constitution was 'patriated' and Canada finally attained legal autonomy. While the provisions of 1867 British North America Act were in large measure retained, the addition of a Charter of Rights and Freedoms represented 'the most radical break ever made in a constitutional and legal tradition hitherto characterized by continuity and incremental change'.[14]

The adoption of the Charter of Rights and Freedoms redefined substantively the way Canadians viewed themselves and their relationship to the governments of Canada. Moreover, the practice of responsible or parliamentary government was altered fundamentally, empowering the Supreme Court of Canada and grounding and amplifying the language of rights in Canadian political discourse. The 1982 Constitution reflects a particular vision of the Canadian political community, a vision closely associated with Pierre Elliot Trudeau. In the words of Peter Russell, this vision consists of 'equal rights-bearing citizens represented in provinces of equal status but expressing their collective national will primarily through the majoritarian institutions of the federal government'.[15]

Such a radical change to the constitutional order touching as it does on the powers of the provincial legislatures would, if conventional practices were followed, require the consent of all provincial governments. The Supreme Court ruled that the 1982 Constitution Act was legally binding on Québec; however, the view from Québec is that the failure to secure its assent renders the process and substance of the constitutional reforms of 1982 illegitimate. The isolation and exclusion of Québec reinforced the perception among Québec francophones that the rest of Canada is insensitive and indifferent to the precariousness of its language and culture in North America. Estranged from the Canadian constitutional order, after two further attempts to reform the constitution, redress for Québec has yet to be attained.

In 1986 the Québec government outlined five conditions for its acceptance of the constitution. The following year the leaders of the provincial and federal government negotiated a package of reforms (known as the Meech Lake Accord), intended to meet Québec's demands. Ratification under the terms of the 1982 Constitution required the approval of the legislatures of the 11 governments. There is general agreement that the Meech Lake Accord failed to secure the requisite consent because (1) the negotiating process, relying as it did on the longstanding practices of executive federalism, was perceived to be undemocratic and the negotiators (the Prime Minister, the ten provincial Premiers, and their advisers) did not adequately represent or 'mirror' the interests and groups in Canadian society; and (2) the substance of the proposed amendments dealt primarily with Québec's demands.

For some this limited 'Québec Round' was deemed to be exclusionary – for example, the constitutional aspirations of the Aboriginal peoples were once again set aside for future consideration. Others feared that the proposed amendments, in particular the recognition of Québec as a distinct society, challenged the principle of equality of provinces, as well as the principle of equal citizenship, because Charter rights could be weakened. Others argued that in meeting the demands made by Québec and extending them to all the provinces, the federal government was weakened significantly.[16]

Drawing on the lessons of this failed effort, a new set of reforms was crafted in 1992 which consciously addressed the criticisms levelled at the content and process of the Meech Lake Accord. The negotiations resulting in the Charlottetown Accord were preceded by extensive public consultations and followed by a consultative referendum. This last attempt at comprehensive reform, widely referred to as the 'Canada Round', sought to be more inclusive than the Meech Lake Accord. Some of the amendments comprised an elected and equal Senate with a suspensive veto on matters of national importance (that is, not quite the so-called 'Triple E' Senate demanded by the West); recogition of the inherent right to self-government for the Aboriginal peoples of Canada; a 'distinct society' clause, defined in terms of Québec's civil code, French language and culture, within the Canada Clause. The Canada Clause sets a list of eight fundamental characteristics intended to guide the courts in their interpretation of the entire constitution, including the Charter of Rights and Freedoms.

Québec was guaranteed at least 25 per cent of the seats in the House of Commons in perpetuity and all provinces were given a veto over future institutional reform (except for the creation of new provinces). This list does not begin to convey the complexity of the proposed changes. The Charlottetown Accord represented an effort to address the legitimate demands of specific members of the federation and at the same time offer safeguards for other members.[17] For instance, the West's demands for Senate reform were partially met (equal and elected but not fully effective) as were concerns for the French language and culture, and Aboriginal and territorial representation by way of a double-majority rule in the Senate for legislation bearing on these issues. Moreover, about one-half of the proposed amendments were not final proposals but guidelines for future negotiations which would have ensured further discussions. In October of 1992 Canadians decisively rejected the package of proposals to 'renew the Canadian federation'.[18]

James Tully likens the predicament facing Canadians to 'being asked to bring the game of hockey into being and learn how to play it as they careened around the ice'.[19] Whereas Janet Ajzenstat, alarmed by the demands for greater and broader public participation in the 'refounding of the country', reminds us that constitutions are understood in liberal democratic theory as 'the rule book for the political game' which should not be changed too frequently or abruptly and 'not by the players while they are on the ice'.[20]

II. Constitutional Democracy

Both democratic theory and constitutionalism are grounded on the notion that every person is worthy of respect by virtue of their status as human beings. Democratic theory looks to popular participation to safeguard this principle, whereas constitutionalism seeks to protect it by limiting legitimate government action. Constitutional democracy requires popular political participation within the limits established by the people themselves. By agreeing to limit their sovereign power, the people place constraints both on the discretionary power of their representatives or government and on future majority decisions.

Constitutional democracy involves more than the rule of law or limited government. The relationship between legality and legitimacy reminds us of the complex weave of historical and cultural forces which create, maintain and at times destroy the fragile consensus that validates a constitutional order. In the process of reforming substantially the constitution, we are impelled to consider what makes such changes morally binding. Insofar as democratic rule requires consent, it is impossible to imagine a situation which could be more demanding of popular consent than rewriting the fundamental rules by which the governed will be governed.

The writing or rewriting of a constitution demands in the first instance the adaptation of general principles to a particular constituency. However, the greater art is 'to bring the constituency to endow the constitution with legitimacy'.[21] In part, the legitimacy of the constitution derives from the capacity of the constituents to recognize as their own the values and ideals enshrined in the text. The art of constitution-making entails the construction of the ideal nation. For those who agree to be bound by the text the constitution is 'not a promise of loyalty to a form of life already realized in the material world but rather a promise of fidelity to an ideal nation'.[22]

The ideal nation they construct for themselves and their progeny is a standard by which to measure the reality of the life they create in common. Thus constitutions are interlaced with hopes and dreams never to be fulfilled in this world, with painfully crafted compromises and unmentionable gaps. All constitutions include such features, they are the 'noble lies' under which we must labour in order to hold out the promise of decency. They also serve another function. In moments when the disjunction between the ideal nation and the real nation, when the gap between what is said to be and what is can no longer be denied or tolerated, the people may be aroused and inspired to renew themselves.

The Canadian public has been aroused by the search for a unifying vision through constitutional reform but the exercise has proved to be exceptionally divisive.[23] The particular challenges of reconstituting Canada are more clearly drawn out by considering the general attributes or functions of constitutions.

III. What are the Functions of a Constitution?

A. The Constitution as Inspiration and Promise

Constitutions implicitly or explicitly (usually in an opening paragraph or preamble) make reference to the fundamental traits of the country which marks it out from all other countries. Indeed, the modern constitutional state demands allegiance by engendering an understanding of the state as a nation. Thus, the constitution, as the supreme law of the land may help to nurture loyalty to the state. It may do so by delineating common or shared values or by expressly recognizing the various constituents which are to be included in the political association.

At present, Canadians are engaged in crafting a comprehensive definition of Canada's 'fundamental characteristics'. This has proved to be highly contentious and is acutely revealing of the underlying principle tension in the Canadian regime: the incompatibility of a uniform pan-Canadian national identity with the demands for recognition of cultural diversity by Québec and the Aboriginal peoples. This tension has run through the whole of the history of Canada, and predates the 1867 agreement which led to the founding of the Canadian federal regime. The constitutional settlement arrived at by the Fathers of Confederation was and is the subject of intense debate. The debate continues because it has profound implications for the way Canadians understand themselves as belonging to Canada.[24]

There are two competing, and perhaps equally valid, ways of answering the question 'Who are the Canadian people?'. Either the Canadian people should be defined in a way that fosters a cohesive, uniform national identity or the Canadian political community must be understood in a way that accommodates and preserves multiple and separate identities. Democratic governance requires an answer to the question 'who are the people' if the democratic promise that sovereignty ultimately rests with the 'people' is to be meaningful. The invention of the 'people' turns on the objective and subject boundaries of citizenship.

Canada redefined itself in the post-war years as an officially bilingual and multicultural country. Increasingly, this conception of the Canadian political community is attacked on a variety of fronts. For the majority of francophones within Québec, including those who are not necessarily supporters of a sovereign Québec, this definition fails to recognize the specificity of Québec. According to this vision of Canada, francophones constitute one of a number of minorities within Canada and while French is recognized as an official language, it is a recognition that divorces language and culture. In other words, language is conceived to be an instrumental tool and not integral to a particular way of life. Thus, it became possible to portray Canada as a country with two official languages and no official cultures.[25]

This vision of Canada is most closely associated with Pierre Elliot Trudeau and his attempts to reconceive the Canadian political community in a way that would undermine the claims of Québec separatists. The concepts of minority/majority, Charles Taylor argues, are both numerical and individualistic in orientation and implications. He explains that these categories apply to individuals as contingent collections of otherwise unrelated individuals. The consequence of this conception is to de-communalizing ethnic communities and depict them as a chance collection of isolated individuals.[26] The Québécois do not apprehend themselves in this way and ultimately, it is their self-definition which must be addressed if we are to move beyond the current impasse.

For Aboriginal peoples, this definition of the Canadian community is an affront as it ignores their existence within the territorial boundaries of Canada, let alone the fact that they are the descendants of the first inhabitants. Many other Canadians are dissatisfied with this understanding of Canada for a variety of reasons; some Canadians regard official bilingualism as creating a burden on them, others impugn the government's multicultural policy as wasteful and divisive.

B. The Constitution as a Charter of Government

A constitution marks the boundaries of the legitimate exercise of power by prescribing the procedures and institutions of governance. The capacities of a democratic regime to manage conflict, especially in deeply divided societies, are influenced by its institutional arrangements. Weaver and Rockman note that, while often indirect and contingent, institutional effects are real and significant. They suggest that institutional reform carries both risks and opportunities, only some of which are predictable given the unique circumstances within which institutions operate. Accordingly, the case for institutional reform should be very strong.[27]

Canadian political institutions include both majoritarian institutions inherited from Britain (parliamentary system) and non-majoritarian institutions that are either indigenous to Canada or adapted from the United States. The basic criticism levelled at Canadian institutional arrangements is that they have failed to manage adequately the longstanding linguistic cleavage and the increasingly significant regional cleavages in Canadian society. Critics also indict the Canadian federal system for failing to live up to the promise of federalism, that is, to accommodate within a single political state deep diversity. However, this expectation needs to be qualified in light of the evidence that federalism can become an instrument of political disintegration or territorial conflict. This can occur if alienated citizens are concentrated in a particular region and if local or regional elites are able to deploy local institutional resources to challenge federal arrangements.[28]

The territorial integrity of Canada is most immediately threatened by the possible separation of Québec from Canada. The option proposed by

Québec nationalists – sovereignty-association – is a response to the failure of the Canadian federal system to accommodate the pervasive belief within Québec that the provincial government requires substantially greater powers to ensure the continued existence of the only viable francophone community in North America. There appears to be broad agreement among francophones that the federal system needs to devolve powers to the Québec government; however, there is a significant difference of opinion among francophones over the extent of the transfer of powers.

A recent survey indicates that there is, among francophone Québeckers, a general willingness to give the government of Québec sole responsibility for the bulk of domestic policies, with the exception of economic policies, about which opinions are either ambivalent or divided.[29] Coupled to Québec's demand for substantial reform of the federal system is the insistence that Québec is recognized *de jure* as a distinct society within Canada. Blais and Nadeau report that even as francophone Québeckers define themselves first as Québeckers, they feel some attachment to Canada. Sovereignty-association can be construed as an attempt to resolve this ambivalence. However, recent opinion polls indicate that Québeckers understand that, regardless of the wording of the referendum question, they are being asked to choose whether or not to separate from Canada.[30]

Blais and Nadeau found that support for sovereignty does *not* result from the belief that Québec has been unfairly treated in the present federal system. They argue that support for sovereignty should be interpreted as the positive assertion of a collective identity rather than a response to some perceived systematic discrimination. Demands for constitutional reform are an attempt to redefine the constitutional and political status of Québec within Canada.

The constitutional reforms required by Québec conflict with the principle of equality of provinces, a principle that is strongly supported outside of Québec and especially in the Western provinces. The latter have been ill-served, for the last quarter century, by an electoral system that seriously underrepresented the citizens of Western Canada in the governing party caucuses of the Canadian House of Commons.[31] The Western provinces seek to offset the clout of the more populous provinces at the federal level by calling for a 'Triple E' (equal, elected and effective) Senate. However, Weaver and others note that there is no guarantee that the West would not be politically isolated or outvoted in a 'Triple E' Senate.

Any accommodation of Québec's demands requires the consent of the other provincial legislatures. In response to the resistance of Canadians outside Québec to the transference of powers to the Québec government, the federal government has proposed to extend to all provinces the provisions sought by Québec. While this response was denounced by the supporters of a strong central government and the 'one nation' vision of Canada, it remains faithful to the principle of the equality of the provinces. Thus, by accommodating Québec's demands, the federal government could be weakened significantly by the wholesale transference of political power to all the provinces.

The practice of symmetrical federalism is perceived within Québec as an insurmountable barrier to accomodating Québec's requirements and the only viable alternative, short of separation, is an asymmetrical arrangement which would avoid the unpopular move towards extensive decentralization. Such a solution would mean that Québec would attain jurisdictional responsibilities not held by other provinces, a situation that offends the vision of a Canada grounded on the principle of the equality of provinces and citizens. By contrast, for Québec it is the preservation and recognition of its difference that is the condition for its inclusion in the Canadian federation.

In addition to the demands of the Western provinces to reform the institutions of the central government and Québec's calls for recognition and devolution, Aboriginal peoples have insisted upon constitutional recognition as distinct peoples and protections for their collective rights and freedoms of self-determination. The inclusion of Aboriginal negotiators and issues in the constitutional reform process was fully evident during the negotiations leading to the Charlottetown Accord. The generous response to Aboriginal demands for distinct status and self-government marks an impressive advance from the not so distant past when the federal government attempted to eliminate Indian status. In 1969 the federal government justified this policy on the grounds that differential status was 'an apartheid-like impediment to Indian advancement'.[32]

Aboriginal peoples vigorously resisted and denounced as assimilationist the imposition of Canadian citizenship. The defeat of this policy was, according to Cairns, a seminal event for it hindered the prospects of pursuing a course of action based on 'the non-recognition of difference and of historical priority'. In time, differential status was extended to all Aboriginals, including the Inuit and the Métis. Aboriginal representatives and issues had been marginal to the debates over reforming the constitution until 1982 when some progress was made; but with the Meech Lake Accord, Aboriginal issues were put aside in order to deal with Québec. However, Aboriginal representatives were involved fully in the multilateral negotiations leading to the Charlottetown Accord wherein they achieved constitutional recognition of their 'inherent right of self-government within Canada' to be exercised as 'one of the three orders of government in Canada'. Moreover, a distinct Aboriginal role or relation in nearly all the major institutions of the Canadian state was secured.

Cairns has offered an explanation for the differential treatment of Québec and Aboriginal claims for cultural recognition in the Charlottetown Accord. He points out that the equality of provinces principle informs the perception outside Québec that Québec is a full participant in the Canadian political system and that the province and citizens of Québec are part of Canada. Additionally, and this should not be underestimated, Cairns notes that special status for Québec is confronted with a theoretically developed federalist discourse, forcefully defended by Trudeau and enshrined in the 1982 Constitution Act.[33] By contrast, self-government for Aboriginal peoples is perceived to be outside of the norm of provincial equality. It is not a denial of the supposedly established relationship among equals because Aboriginal peoples have long been marginal to the Canadian sense of self and in the Canadian political system.

C. The Constitution as a Charter of Fundamental Human Rights

A Bill of Rights is intended to protect citizens or individuals from the potential abuse by the government or a majority. This conventional understanding fails to admit that bills of rights serve an important declaratory function as a statement of ideals. A quick perusal of bills of rights across Western liberal democracies indicates that, aside from the rights and freedoms historically defined within the liberal tradition as fundamental, there are other rights, more in the nature of privileges and immunities, that are relevant to the particular political community within which they are intended to function. This latter category of rights are the form by which the values and needs that sustain the political community are negotiated to allow a collectivity to live in relative peace. Contrary to the popular belief that rights should never be negotiated, political communities and individuals are impelled repeatedly to evaluate the meaning of rights and to measure them against what their experiences reveal.

The rights and freedoms enshrined in a bill of rights demarcate the public and private spheres. Individual rights (the obvious and most cited example being the privatization of religious belief), 'privatize' certain issues so as to protect them from potentially oppressive majorities and immunize them from public scrutiny and debate. The exclusion of irresolvable or emotionally charged issues from public debate is defended most often on the grounds that this is conducive to the stability of democratic governance.

In a sense, the citizens have agreed to place a limit on what can be debated publicly, just as they have agreed to limit their sovereign powers by adhering to a constitution. The counterclaim, attributed to Hannah Arendt, is that deliberation over fundamental political questions may be both liberating and ennobling.

In Canada the entrenchment of a Charter of Rights and Freedoms in the 1982 Constitutional Act has contributed to the broadening of participation in the constitutional reform process. It is recognized generally that the Charter has been an instrument of democratization which has nurtured a participant political culture.[34] In principle this is a desirable change, in practice it has exacerbated the opposition between proponents of a uniform conception of citizenship and those who demand that deep diversity be accommodated within the Canadian polity. The multiple effects of this reform to the Canadian constitution attest to Rockman and Weaver's warning, noted above, that there are both risks and opportunities associated with institutional reform. Canadian scholars were well aware that the entrenchment of a Charter of Rights would empower significantly the judiciary; however, they failed miserably in assuming that the strong tradition of judicial self-restraint prior to 1982 meant it would be improbable that the Canadian Supreme Court would match the judicial activism of their American counterparts.[35]

The introduction of the Charter redefined the relationship between citizens and the state and, following Cairns, it is widely recognized that the Charter has opened up an alternative dialogue that sits uncomfortably with the established political discourse of federal–provincial politics. Scholars did not appreciate fully how the shift from subjects to rights-bearing citizens would open to question the locus of sovereignty in Canada. In practice, this question has been debated in terms of who should participate and to what extent in the process of constitutional reform.

A further consequence of the Charter, the direct result of the fact that it is binding on both the federal and provincial governments, is that it limits provincial variations that fail to comply with a Charter protected right. While federal legislation is liable also to Charter nullification, the Charter affirms uniform Canadian values, and privileges these values over territorially based or local particularisms.

The inclusion of a legislative override was conceded to secure support from provincial premiers cognizant that their powers would be diminished by an entrenched Charter of Rights. This provision, decried by Charter supporters, is a pragmatic compromise that may be seen as giving Canada the best of British and American constitutionalism. The advantage of the override clause is that it permits the citizenry, through their accountable and responsible representatives, to reverse the judicial ruling on a rights issue without resorting to formal constitutional amendment. The override clause can be used only under fairly stringent conditions and in exceptional cases; for example, once adopted, the override is valid for a limited period whereupon it must be renewed, allowing for further public debate. Moreover, the 'notwithstanding clause' has the potential to qualify somewhat the nationalizing effects of the Charter by bringing local or regional standards to bear upon rights issues.

Not only has the Charter been widely embraced in Canada outside Québec, it has altered the political culture within the 'Rest of Canada' by authorizing the principle that individual rights are universal attributes that belong equally to all citizens of Canada. The commitment to this classical liberal egalitarianism places a formidable impediment to the notion that justice may require the recognition and preservation of difference. The antipathy among elites in Québec to the Canadian Charter of Rights is not based on a rejection of liberal rights *per se*, but to the political purposes of the Charter in thwarting the aspirations of Québec within the federation. The negotiations among the first ministers which led to the adoption of the 1982 Constitution is seen as a notorious instance of the 'betrayal' of Québec. In this sense the Charter is tainted by its association with Trudeau (the nemesis of nationalists of all hues in Québec), the humiliation of Lévesque (the beloved founder of the Parti Québécois) and the apparent dirty dealings that led to 'the night of the long knives'.

The applicability of the Charter to future Aboriginal governments is contested within the Aboriginal communities. Opposition from the main bodies representing Aboriginal nations is based on the perception that the Charter is alien to the traditions and practices of conflict–resolution and decision-making indigenous to Aboriginal culture and as such, it is potentially an instrument of assimilation. None the less, there is dissent within the Aboriginal community to this position. The most vocal have been a group of Aboriginal women represented by the Native Women's Association of Canada. In the most recent round of constitutional negotiations, the NWAC argued for separate representation for native women. They claimed that other Aboriginal organizations (which included native women in their delegations) were insensitive to the risk to equality rights faced by Aboriginal women if the Canadian Charter of Rights and Freedoms was not made to apply to future Aboriginal governments. The NWAC represent Aboriginal women who lost their Indian status through marriage to non-Natives, regained it under federal law but, they claim, all too often they are unable to regain band membership or live on reserves because of opposition from male leaders on the reserves. They believe themselves to be so vulnerable that they do not want the 'notwithstanding clause' of the Charter to be available to future Aboriginal governments.[36]

As a nation-building device, the Charter has fallen short of inculcating loyalty to the larger Canadian community because of the insistance that every Canadian citizen belong to the federation in precisely the same way. The two subsequent attempts to reform comprehensively the basic law of the land have demonstrated that a new constitutional culture has developed.

In part this new order draws sustenance from increasing demands for greater opportunities to participate in reconstituting the country. The participation of various organized political interests in drafting the wording of the Charter marked the coming of age of what are now commonly referred to as 'Charter groups'.

The Charter groups include those groups who successfully lobbied to ensure recognition in the Charter – women, official-language minorities, multicultural groups, the handicapped, the aged as well as a more disparate grouping of individuals whose vision of Canada entails first and foremost the protection of rights as enshrined in the Charter. Cairns was the first to recognize that Charter groups have developed a proprietary attitude to the interpretation and development of 'their' clause. Given that future changes to the constitution require the approval of the federal and provincial legislatures, these groups have understood that their Charter rights are dependent upon governments refraining from abusing their monopoly of the amending power.[37] Perhaps Tocqueville's observation that envy is an endogenous vice of democracies can be detected in the resistance of these groups to extending recognition to other constituent members of the federation. All the same these constitutional interest groups have been at the forefront of a more 'participant-oriented constitutional culture' which has profound implications for finding a way through the current impasse.

IV. How is the Constitution Changed Validly?

The first distinction to draw is between ordinary amendments that are made under the procedures of an established constitution and the fundamental alteration of the constitutional regime, the founding or refounding of a political association. A second distinction with regard to comprehensive constitutional change is reform at the level of institutional arrangements or regime change and reform to the fundamental shape of the body politic or political association. For example, the French have had 16 constitutions from 1791 to 1958 but throughout, the existence of France as a nation/nationality has not been questioned. Despite three republics since 1875 (the Third, Fourth, Fifth Republic), France has remained 'La République'. Consider another example which demonstrates this same point. From 1940 to 1945 France included the forces of de Gaulle in England and those in France who resisted the German occupation: the rest, Vichy, were 'foreign to the idea, and to the words, of France'.[38]

As should be evident, the objective of constitutional reform over the last 30 years is the reconstruction of the idea of Canada. These efforts to reconstitute Canada have precipitated a debate on first principles. We find ourselves in relatively unchartered terrain. Liberal theory does justify the 'right to revolt' under conditions where government has become so defective that abolishment or alteration is justified. Obviously this does not apply to Canada. Ajzenstat reminds us that liberal theory warns against popular participation in drawing up a new constitution. Ajzenstat denies the existence of a democratic right to participate in constitution-making. It is fitting to consider the implications of allowing greater public participation in the agenda-setting and negotiation phases of the constitutional reform process, as the traditional practices of elite accommodation are no longer acceptable.

The pressing question is how to meet the requirements of political equality and ensure thoughtful deliberation on complex issues under conditions that do not lend themselves to interactive deliberation. The securing of consent has become more difficult as the meaning of representation, the form and scope of political participation, the relevant constituency whose consent is necessary and whose participation is required is contested. David Held considers the challenge posed to these 'key ideas of democracy' in a world of regional and global interconnectedness to demonstrate the limitations of democratic governance within a nation-state. While Held is concerned with democratic relations among states as a requisite for meaningful democracy within states, I believe that these same questions bear, as they always have, on democratic governance within states and take on even more urgency in reconstituting the fundamental law of a country under post-modern conditions.[39]

The amending formula endorsed in the 1982 Constitution Act is based on a vision of Canada as a federal regime, yet the inclusion of a Charter of Rights and Freedoms enhances the status of citizens and strengthens the idea of a pan-Canadian community of equal rights-bearing citizens. These contradictory components locate sovereignty both in the representatives of the people in their respective provinces and the federal government and in the people themselves. The constitution itself created the conditions in which subsequent reform efforts would be criticized on the grounds that participation had been exclusionary and elitist.

The complicated set of amending procedures are highly federalized – relying principally on securing the consent of provincial legislatures and the federal parliament; the requisite degree of consent varies from unanimity to unilateral and bilateral agreements depending on the subject-matter and the governments involved. These provisions apply to the ratification phase. The Constitution is silent on how proposed amendments are to be devised.

The change in ratification procedures meant that, in practice, there would be some debate and a vote in the major democratic representative bodies across the country. This is a notable change from closed First Ministers Conferences. These conferences, a staple of executive federalism, have always included the prime minister and the premiers of the ten provinces representing 'their' governments and regardless of their party affiliations, the prime minister and the premiers are cast in adversary roles.[40] While the 1982 Constitution moved the ratification process from executives to the legislatures, the agenda-setting and bargaining phases of the constitutional reform process remained the purview of the first ministers until this convention was challenged explicitly during the ratification phase of the Meech Lake Accord. Substantial efforts were made to overcome some of the deficiencies of the process and content of the Meech Lake Accord.

The process of constitutional reform culminating in a national referendum on the Charlottetown Accord represents the best effort to date to include 'ordinary' Canadians. The 'Canada round' is best understood in terms of Peter Russell's arresting metaphor of the hourglass. The top part of the hourglass represents the public consultation phase when most of the proposals in the Charlottetown Accord were debated. The public consultations from mid 1990 to the spring of 1992 included three federally sponsored consultations and five national conferences; Aboriginal peoples conducted four consultations and the territorial governments consulted their constituents. Some of these consultations were monopolized by non-elected spokespersons from business, labour, special interest groups, and other large associations. Despite populist pretensions, exercises in public consultation are hijacked all too often by intelligent, articulate and unaccountable elites. On a more positive note, interested citizens had an opportunity to garner information through the wide media coverage and televised sessions of these hearings.

In the next phase, the hourglass narrows as the process reverts to executive federal negotiations. These multilateral negotiations were expanded to include ministers from the two territorial governments and representatives from four national Aboriginal organizations. Notably, Québec was not represented at these negotiations as the premier of Québec insisted on receiving from the rest of Canada an 'offer' before engaging in negotiations. The hourglass narrows further when the final terms of the Charlottetown Accord were negotiated by first ministers. The bottom part of the hourglass represents the referendum campaign. The referendum campaign lasted less than two months at the end of which voters were asked to vote for or against the first ministers' agreement.

Were Canadians given ample opportunity to fully and genuinely deliberate on a proposal that would reconstitute their country? The short answer is no. Canadians were asked to express an opinion on a prepared package of reforms. The referendum campaign was conducted in the manner of an electoral campaign and the vote was an aggregation of individual preferences. However, the rejection of the Charlottetown Accord does not indicate necessarily that Canadians did not understand what was being proposed. Alain Noël has put forward a compelling case, based on a re-examination of the empirical evidence and the requirements of deliberation, that Canadians were not ignorant of their self-interest or about the principles of justice they believed should form the basis of their life in common. He argues that Canadians could not discover, amid the conflicting ideas of equality and by extension the contradictory visions of Canada in the proposed constitutional package, a clear conception of justice.[41]

The Charlottetown Accord reflected rather than resolved the competing and multiple visions of Canada. To the extent that Noël's interpretation of the 1992 referendum is valid, it belies the assumption that citizens in contemporary liberal democracies, habituated to minding their own business, are not engaged or aroused sufficiently to deliberate. But even if Noël provides a positive interpretation of the referendum, he concedes that the process of deliberation was limited. A characteristic feature of a truly deliberative process is that initial preferences or opinions are transformed through a process that incorporates the views of others. Deliberation, in this sense, presumes that individuals are open to rational arguments and that they are capable of setting aside their particular interests to arrive at an agreed judgment. This is only possible if participants trust one another.

While research in small group contexts indicates that trust can be cultivated through discussion itself, it is unclear how the low levels of trust among Canadians and between Canadian citizens and their political representatives can be built up.[42] Distrust of political elites and fellow citizens has encouraged more groups to secure 'in writing', through constitutional provisions, guarantees that once might have been granted informally or through regular legislation. The weak bonds of trust are a formidable impediment for a country that has no alternative, short of breakup, but to learn to live with deep diversity. What remains to be seen is whether the desire to live together in one country is strong enough to impel Canadians to endeavour to discover a form of justice that would preserve and promote the diversity that is Canada.

NOTES

1. Janet Ajzenstat contrasts this situation in the West today with the desire in Eastern Europe and the former Soviet Union to embrace competitive political parties and interest groups to represent different sectors of society. See Janet Ajzenstat, 'Constitution Making and the Myth of the People', in Curtis Cooke (ed.), *Constitutional Predicament: Canada after the Referendum of 1992* (Montreal: McGill-Queen's University Press, 1994), p.124.
2. Sheldon S. Wolin, 'Democracy, Difference and Re-Cognition', *Political Theory*, Vol.21, No.3 (1993), p.468.
3. Clifford Geertz, 'The Uses of Diversity', *Michigan Quarterly Review*, Vol.25, No.1 (1986), p.121.

4. Constitutional politics at the mega level differs from normal constitutional politics in that the former is concerned with forging a consensus on the very nature of the political community, its identity and fundamental principles; secondly, mega constitutional politics by its very nature is highly charged and emotional. Peter Russell, *Constitutional Odyssey: Can Canadians Become a Sovereign People?*, 2nd edn. (Toronto: University of Toronto Press, 1993), p.75.
5. See Charles Taylor, 'Shared and Divergent Values', in Guy Laforest (ed.), *Reconciling the Solitudes: Essays on Canadian Federalism and Nationalism* (Montreal: McGill-Queen's University Press, 1993), pp.155–86.
6. Donald Smiley,' The Canadian Charter of Rights and Freedoms with Special Emphasis on Québec-Canada Relations', in William R. McKercher (ed.), *The U.S. Bill of Rights and the Canadian Charter of Rights and Freedoms* (Toronto: Ontario Economic Council, 1983), p.223.
7. See Guy Lachapelle, Gérald Bernier, Daniel Salée and Luc Bernier, *The Québec Democracy: Structures, Processes and Policies* (Toronto: McGraw-Hill Ryerson, 1993), pp.73–93.
8. The PQ first gained office in the fall of 1976 and held the first referendum on sovereignty-association in May 1980. Sixty per cent of all voters and 52 per cent of francophones voted no to a question which asked voters to give the Québec government a mandate to negotiate sovereignty-association with Canada. Despite this defeat the PQ went on to hold power until 1985 and was reelected in September of 1994. A second referendum is promised this autumn.
9. James Tully, 'Diversity's Gambit Declined', in Cooke (ed), *Constitutional Predicament*, p.150.
10. For a thoughtful analysis of the possibility that the imposition of collective identity on heterogeneous populations may have exhausted itself see Gregory Jusdanis, 'Beyond National Culture?', *Boundary 2*, Vol.22, No.1 (1995), pp.23–60; for a cautiously optimistic reading of the current impasse, see Tully, 'Diversity's Gambit Declined'.
11. Geertz, p.122.
12. Alan C. Cairns, 'Constitutional Change and the Three Equalities' in Douglas E. Williams (ed.), *Reconfigurations: Canadian Citizenship and Constitutional Change* (Toronto: McClelland & Stewart, 1995), pp.216–37.
13. This position is clearly spelled out in Barry Cooper, 'Looking Eastward, Looking Backward: A Western Reading of the Never-Ending Story', in Cooke (ed.), *Constitutional Predicament*, pp.89–108.
14. Smiley, p.220.
15. Russell, pp.125–6.
16. See David E. Smith, Peter MacKinnon and John C. Courtney (eds.), *After Meech Lake: Lessons for the Future* (Saskatoon, Saskatchewan: Fifth House Publishers, 1991).
17. Tully, pp.154–5.
18. Among voters in Québec 56.7 per cent voted no; outside Québec 54.3 per cent voted no. The Aboriginal vote is less reliable because the count provided by the Assembly of First Nations comes from reservation polling stations and may include non-Aboriginal voters and excludes Aboriginal voters who voted outside the reservations. With these qualifications in mind, the reported no vote among Aboriginal voters was 62.1 per cent. It is estimated that 74.9 per cent of eligible voters across Canada voted; this is consistent with the rate of turnout for federal elections. See Curtis Cooke, 'Introduction: Canada's Predicament' in *Constitutional Predicament: Canada after the Referendum of 1992*, p.7. The *Consensus Report on the Constitution, Charlottetown, August 28, 1992* (the Charlottetown Accord) sets out in 20 pages and six chapters proposals intended to culminate, as stated in the preface, in the 'renewal of the Canadian federation'. The text is reprinted in Cooke, *Constitutional Predicament*, pp.226–49.
19. Tully, p.153.
20. Ajzenstat, p.113.
21. Daniel J. Elazar, 'Constitution-making: The Pre-eminently Political Act', in Keith G. Banting and Richard Simeon (eds.), *Redesigning the State: The Politics of Constitutional Change*, (Toronto: University of Toronto Press, 1985), p.232.
22. Anne Norton, *Republic of Signs: Liberal Theory and American Popular Culture* (Chicago,

IL: University of Chicago Press, 1993), p.132.
23. For a particularly revealing account of the competing visions of Canada see Jeffrey Simpson, *Faultlines: Struggling for a Canadian Vision* (Toronto: HarperCollins, 1994).
24. For an insightful analysis of this debate see Samuel V. LaSelva, 'Re-imagining Confederation: Moving Beyond the Trudeau–Levesque Debate', *Canadian Journal of Political Science*, Vol.26, No.4 (1993), pp.699–20.
25. Rainer Knopff, 'Language and Culture in the Canadian Debate: The Battle of the White Papers', *Canadian Review of Studies in Nationalism*, Vol.6 (1979), pp.66–82.
26. Taylor, p.172.
27. R. Kent Weaver and Bert A. Rockman (eds.), *Do Institutions Matter?:Government Capabilities in the United States and Abroad* (Washington: The Brookings Institution, 1993), p.39.
28. Weaver and Rockman, pp.296–9; Allen Kornberg and Harold D. Clarke, *Citizens and Community: Political Support in a Representative Democracy* (New York: Cambridge University Press, 1992), pp.256–60.
29. André Blais and Richard Nadeau, 'To Be or Not To Be Sovereigntist?: Québeckers' Perennial Dilemma', *Canadian Public Policy*, Vol.18, No.1 (1992), p.100.
30. *The Montreal Gazette*, Friday, 17 Feb. 1995 pp.A1–A2.
31. R. Kent Weaver, 'Political Institutions and Canada's Constitutional Crisis', in R. Kent Weaver (ed.), *The Collapse of Canada* (Washington, DC: The Brookings Institute, 1992), p.70.
32. Cairns, p.326.
33. Allen C. Cairns, 'The Charlottetown Accord: Multinational Canada v. Federalism', in Curtis Cook (ed.), *Constitutional Predicament*, p.59.
34. Alan C. Cairns, *Charter versus Federalism: The Dilemmas of Constitutional Reform* (Montreal: McGill-Queen's University Press, 1992), p.4. Charles Taylor provides a cogent counterargument in *Reconciling the Solitudes*, pp.87–109.
35. F.L. Morton, 'Judicial Politics Canadian Style: The Supreme Court's Contribution to the Constitutional Crisis of 1992', in Curtis Cook (ed.), *Constitutional Predicament*, pp.135–6.
36. Cairns, *Reconfigurations*, pp.210–14.
37. Cairns, *Charter versus Federalism*, p.6.
38. Norton, p.131.
39. David Held, 'Democracy: From City-State to Cosmopolitan Order?', in David Held (ed.), *Prospects for Democracy* (Oxford: Polity Press, 1993), pp.26–7.
40. Kornberg and Clarke, p.103.
41. Alain Noël, 'Deliberating a Constitution: The Meaning of the Canadian Referendum of 1992', in Curtis Cooke (ed), *Constitutional Predicament*, pp.74–5.
42. David Miller, 'Deliberative Democracy and Social Choice', in David Held (ed.), *Prospects for Democracy*, pp.83–4, 88.

The Messenger as Policy Maker: Thinking About the Press and Policy Networks in the Washington Community

ADRIENNE M. JAMIESON

Social scientists have shed considerable light on the ways in which the press as 'the fourth branch' of government collaborates with policy-makers in the other three branches to produce a constant stream of messages, most of which are directed towards others in the Washington policy community. This study suggests that this message game can be viewed as a conversation which occurs within policy networks, facilitated by the press. The press interpret and transmit messages sent by participants in the network which reflect the needs of policy-makers, their institutional bases and the myriad cultural forces in the Washington community. These messages are also shaped by reporters who are themselves specialists in the discourse of the policy networks captured by their newsbeats. Reporters craft stories which reflect the norms of their profession, the needs of their news organizations and the political culture of Washington. The growing number of participants in policy discourse and the increased role played by specialty publications, on-line services and local news programmes have contributed to the fluidity of policy networks while at the same time enabling adept participants to send messages through alternative pathways. Cynicism about political institutions may be exacerbated by this system in part because citizens do not have the information necessary to decode these messages.

The Fourth Branch and the Other Three

In 1959, Douglass Cater argued that in a system based on the separation of powers, the press serve both as a means of communication between the branches of government (for example, carrying messages between policy-makers) and as a 'day-to-day measure of public opinion' for politicians and bureaucrats.[1] Cater suggested that reporters are more than mere 'recorders' of government and are in fact also full-fledged participants in the business of government and politics. He described a number of the roles played by the press that remain at the core of what we observe today: choosing among 'myriad events which seethe beneath the surface' (agenda-setting); illuminating policy, giving it 'sharpness and clarity or prematurely exposing it as with an undeveloped film, causing its destruction' (explaining and interpreting government actions); and at its worst 'operating with arbitrary and faulty standards as an agent of disorder and confusion while at its best exerting a creative influence on Washington politics' (proposing frameworks).[2]

In the decades since Cater's analysis, political scientists have continued to view the role of the press as the 'fourth branch' in the politics and policy-making of Washington. These efforts have shed considerable light on the ways in which the press in essence collaborates with government policy-makers to produce a constant stream of messages, some intended for consumption by a mass audience, but most directed towards others in Washington who have a professional stake in the policy at hand. Bernard Cohen's classic exploration of the ways in which journalists interact with policy-makers in the foreign affairs community laid the groundwork for thinking more precisely about the press as an institution in and of itself and the specific roles reporters play as messengers in the political system.[3] Cohen stresses that journalists are authentic participants in foreign policy-making because they are not mere mechanical purveyors of factual information. That is, professional norms, shared values and the organizational dynamics of the news media all affect what ultimately appears in the media. Policy-makers depend upon the news for understanding the world (that is, the Washington community as well as the public) in which they operate. They interpret messages crafted by other policy-makers and shaped by the press. They view the press as a 'useful handmaiden' in the competition over policies, a powerful way to themselves exert influence. There are inevitable tensions in this policy-maker–journalist relationship which Cohen and others have noted – when the norms and work routines of journalism clash with politicians' needs to communicate a message ungarbled by the press. But even as policy-makers publicly complain about the intrusion of the press and the effects of negative coverage, in private they view the press as a resource necessary to do their jobs.[4]

Exploring specific aspects of this collaborative relationship between the press and the three other branches of government continues to yield insights into the nature and significance of reporter–policy-maker relations. Studies have documented how different political institutions arrange their dealings with the press and the ways in which they send messages that reflect their role in the political system. Presidents gravitate towards public speeches and ceremonies because these activities can be orchestrated entirely by their own efforts. These sorts of strategies reflect the primary advantages presidents have over other policy-makers – the news comes to them. The President is by definition an authoritative source and, as an individual, the President is 'easier' to write about than complex institutions like the US Congress or the federal bureaucracy. The problem for presidents is attempting to control the media's version of their messages and to limit the flow of conflicting messages in the form of leaks or statements made by other authoritative sources with alternative agendas. Yet these sorts of risks are deemed acceptable because presidents are compelled to get their message out – especially when they are unable to accomplish their goals in other ways.[5]

The organizational response to the need for strategic communication has been to increase the size of the White House Office of Communications, but more importantly to enhance the role of news management in virtually all aspects of White House decision-making.[6] In recent separate accounts of policy-making in the Clinton White House, Elizabeth Drew and Bob Woodward both describe the ways in which campaign and media consultants have become active participants in just about every policy discussion.[7] In other words, the distinction between policy-making and news-making has virtually disappeared. In spite of these efforts, presidents are not always successful. As Sam Kernell shows, contextual factors such as the state of the economy and the president's popularity may thwart ordinarily successful media strategies.[8] Certainly there is much evidence to suggest that Clinton's efforts with the media have not enabled him to overcome low approval ratings.[9]

News-making is closely tied to policy-making in Congress as well, but the complexity of an institution composed of 535 individuals means that the news media must find their own ways to focus and simplify their efforts. All members of Congress are not equal in the eyes of the national press. They are most interested in party leaders, Senators and a handful of committee chairs who have reputations as players in Washington. For most members, the only consistent media relationship they have is with their hometown press. One of the best ways to send a message to a member is through stories and editorials in the local press because many members view local news media as proxies for their constituents' opinions.[10] These communications take on added strength when they appear on the member's desk along with concurring editorials in elite newspapers like *The New York Times* and *The Washington Post*. Messages through the local press flow both ways. Senator Paul Simon (a former newspaper editor) says that he telephones Illinois newspaper editors when he 'needs a helping hand', but notes that if he were to do this too often, it would lose its value.[11]

But as Richard Fenno has shown, re-selection is not the only goal for most members. Some seek a role in making national policy or strive to build up a reputation which will enable them to run for higher office. These members compete for coverage in all sorts of forums, including the Sunday morning news shows, habitually watched by Washington 'insiders' or for invitations to speak at visible policy conferences sponsored by prominent think-tanks or universities which are often covered by the national and the elite policy press such as *National Journal* or *Congressional Quarterly*.[12] Occasionally an entrepreneurial member uses the press to define an issue or a cause in such a way as to force other members to act – a particularly impressive feat given the natural propensity in Congress for inaction. For example, House Republican leader Newt Gingrich, then a rank-and-file member, used repeated appearances on *C-SPAN* (speaking to an empty House chamber beyond the camera's range) to launch ethics charges against then Speaker Jim Wright, while planting the idea that 'corruption' had spread beyond the Speaker to Congress as an institution. Accompanied by a persistent flow of press releases and letters to the local as well as the national press, Gingrich slowly convinced other members with the support of journalists not only to oust the Speaker, but also to echo his calls for congressional reform.[13]

The interaction between the press and executive branch agencies reflects the differing needs and interests of Cabinet secretaries, long-term bureaucrats and the Presidential branch.[14] Bureaucrats and political appointees generally labour in relative obscurity unless they orchestrate press coverage, often by providing an alternative version of the news from that offered by the President. These conflicts, some real, some invented, may be marketed to the press in the form of leaks or trial balloons in an effort to test the waters for a specific policy proposal or they may reflect real conflicts within agencies over policy. Pentagon officials, unhappy with the Clinton administration's intention to lift the ban on gays in the military, leaked a confidential memorandum written by then Defense Secretary Les Aspin to CBS correspondent Bob Schieffer. Schieffer had already scheduled Aspin for an appearance on the Sunday morning news show *Face the Nation* when he received the memorandum 'over the transom' and his resulting questioning of Aspin not only signalled impending action, but the administration's failure to come up with a politically viable strategy. The story spilled over into Monday morning's papers and a number of politicians, military leaders and interest groups jumped into the fray.[15] A *Washington Post* story revealed that Alice Sessions, the wife of then FBI Director William Sessions used an FBI car and driver to go shopping in New York while her husband attended a meeting. The story was not the result of enterprising reporting, but of tips from individuals within the FBI who wanted to embarrass the Director. Post reporters deemed the story newsworthy in part because Sessions' job was already in jeopardy – he was being investigated by the Justice Department's Office of Professional Responsibility, giving the story a context which meshed with the Washington community's collective assessment that Sessions' days as FBI Director were numbered.[16]

Contrived splits between the President and Cabinet members can also be used to test policy if the news reinforces the notion of the Cabinet member as a 'true believer' who can always be portrayed as thwarting the President.

The extent to which the White House, members of Congress and various participants across government agencies have multiple and conflicting agendas for a given policy area means that coordinating media strategies from federal agencies is a challenge that is not easily met organizationally. In his study of press operations in various federal agencies, Stephen Hess found that press officers are generally 'spokesmen without influence' who are there to provide information in reporters' language.[17] Policy-makers have plenty of incentives to develop and send their own messages, regardless of efforts to coordinate strategies.

There is a smattering of evidence that even Supreme Court justices are conscious of the need to send and receive messages through the press. Justices are very much a part of the Washington community and like others in it read newspapers with an eye to decoding messages sent by other policy-makers and gauging public opinion.[18] But unlike the other branches, the Supreme Court is covered largely through its own documents and on its own time schedule. When decisions are reached, the Public Information Office issues copies of the text, but no press releases are provided and no press conferences or interviews are held. Leaks seldom occur because much of the discussion surrounding decisions is confined to the nine justices and their clerks who are sworn to secrecy.[19] Justices occasionally have opportunities to send messages before decisions are reached by asking questions during oral arguments in ways that will attract media coverage. Some analysts argue that recent increases in individually-written opinions reflect a growing interest on the part of Justices to express their views to others in the Washington community and the public. So while Supreme Court justices do not explicitly acknowledge that they have a media strategy, they transmit and receive messages through the press in ways that reflect the organizational design of the Court and its role in the Washington community and the larger political system.

These quick snapshots of the institutional approach to press–government interactions explain a great deal about the way messages are sent, received and interpreted in the Washington community. However, since Cater's and Cohen's analyses, there are more players and interests, accompanied by more and different norms and routines than can be accounted for by examining how each of the three 'branches' interacts with the fourth. The roster of participants in the Washington message game has expanded well beyond the boundaries of the political institutions described above to include public interest groups; trade and professional associations; think-tanks; political consultants and pundits with an interest in national affairs.[20] So for any given issue, policy-making is best described as a conversation among an array of participants – some within government, some outside of government. The outcome of this conversation may emerge in the form of legislation or some other governmental action or it may be the generation of a 'new' policy problem and the development of language and frameworks to describe and analyse it. A good portion of this conversation is mediated by the press, ebbing and flowing over time as issues and their champions vie for Washington's attention.

Policy Networks: Conversation and Expertise

How do we begin to think about the press in a way which captures both the institutional and conversational aspects of policy-making in the American political system? Policy networks may provide one approach. Policy or issue networks; sub-governments, as Cater called them, or epistemic communities are terms that all capture the idea that groups of issue specialists construct themselves around a policy-making dialogue.[21] The individuals in these networks define the frameworks and the language in which a given policy is discussed; they circumscribe the acceptable solutions; and they compete among themselves to expand and shape the network itself not only to secure preferred results, but also to shape the discourse within the Washington community and beyond. All of these individuals have multiple identities in the Washington community which, together with special knowledge of a particular issue area, affect their views and approaches to policy. These identities arise from the institutional bases discussed above, geographic ties, generational influences and specialized training. The ways in which individuals bring all of these influences to bear on a particular policy set the tone of the network.[22] Foreign policy networks, for example, tend to be built around issue specialists who have for the most part attended a handful of elite universities. They have spent their careers moving within and among a handful of government positions and elite think-tanks or professional associations (for example, the Council on Foreign Relations, the Carnegie Endowment, the Brookings Institution). Individuals are valued for their expertise and may find themselves serving as advisers in both Republican and Democratic administrations. The conversation within these networks is based more on expertise in particular geographic areas than on partisan distinctions.[23]

Reporters too are participants in these policy networks. From an organizational perspective, news beats are issue-oriented so reporters move within networks of specialists as they gather news. Journalists also make choices as they go about their work – choices about what ought to be covered and how and whom to consult in the process. In other words, reporters select which messages to transmit from among policy-makers and how to interpret or frame them. In the process, reporters filter the messages policy-makers send in ways that affect the nature of the conversation within

120   DEMOCRACY AND NORTH AMERICA

the network, ultimately shaping and reshaping the network itself by enticing
others to engage in a policy discussion they had previously ignored or by
proposing alternative approaches that lead to a reconfiguration of interests.
Others in the Washington community and in some instances the public –
those beyond the specialized policy community – are essentially consumers
of the distant message who may choose to engage in the discussion if the
message signals them in some way. If the business of policy networks is
conversation, then virtually all of the activity within these networks is
'journalistic'.[24]

Cultural forces also shape the policy dialogue and they are captured
more readily in an analysis of communication within issue networks than
from the vantage point of a single political institution. One way to think
about political culture is in terms of the way people concoct frameworks for
organizing contemporary events based on shared views of history.[25] Many of
these frameworks are brought in from the wider Washington community.
Conversations within policy networks are often about applying issues to
existing frameworks – a process which enables policy-makers to foist 'new'
issues on to the agenda as they crop up. So the Clinton administration's
'Goals 2000' package, passed by Congress and conceived of within the
education policy network as a first step toward educational reform, later
reappears as federal intrusion into local schools as new participants (for
example, new Republican members of Congress and representatives of the
Christian Coalition) enter the conversation, bringing new frameworks with
them. Frameworks are also created within networks as myriad cultural
forces affect the language, symbols and ideas which participants in the
process invoke.

Michael Cornfield has described this process as 'negotiating a
discourse', an arrangement for regular communication about a topic. His
description fits the sorts of conversations we observe in policy networks.
Cornfield notes that what he refers to as discourse participants develop a set
of conventions for their conversations including: an array of perennial
subtopics; jargon (for faster and for the uninitiated, often difficult to
comprehend exchanges); etiquette (for smoother relations among
participants); a canon (a collection of texts considered to be central to their
conversation); an elite (a sub-set of participants whose actions and words
attract special notice; myths (frameworks, shared beliefs which help a
discourse to cohere in the midst of numerous other conversations and a
changing world); and rhetoric (a prevalent style of persuasion). Cornfield
describes discourse rhetoric as a craft – participants know how to attract
attention from others in the network and how to increase the chances that
their messages will be willingly received both by the press and other policy-
makers. They are conversant with the current 'big stories' and can apply

them to the relevant myths or frameworks. They can invoke phrases from 'canonical works' – which may be speeches, books or historical documents, well known among network participants. They abide by the etiquette of the network in the ways they stage events and leak information, using jargon where appropriate in their messages to signal others of their intentions.[26] So participants in policy networks are not only substantive issue specialists; they are also experts in a distinctive domain of discourse.

Journalists too are 'discourse experts' in the policy conversations encompassed by their news beats. The press pick and choose strands of the conversation, sometimes transmitting messages between regular communicators in the jargon only they really understand and at other times interpreting insider messages for the larger Washington community or the public. These conversations never really end – no one has the 'last word'. The institutions of the press help to sustain this continuing discussion by providing forums that enable these messages to be sent and received.

Gregg Easterbrook's recent study of environmentalism, *A Moment on the Earth*, illustrates how environmental policy networks are 'fogbound in woe', populated by environmentalists who continually proclaim emergencies and crises even when the data do not support them. What binds this diverse group of issue specialists together (scientists, lawyers, engineers and economists) is a shared framework or belief that not only do we face a number of dire environmental crises, but also that we should downplay scientific findings of environmental improvement because good news could dilute a sense of public anxiety supporting political action.[27] Policy-makers have conducted sustained conversations on a wide range of topics from acid rain to the spotted owl based on this framework for over two decades. Easterbrook quotes Vice President Gore as describing the US environmental situation as 'extremely grave – the worst crisis our country has ever faced.' Former Senate Majority Leader George Mitchell, the force behind the 1990 Clean Air Act is quoted as declaring that 'we risk turning our world into a lifeless desert'. Former Senator Gaylord Nelson (later director of the Wilderness Society) is quoted as saying that current environmental problems 'are a greater threat to the Earth's life sustaining systems than a nuclear war.'[28] Easterbrook describes this discourse as 'theatrical' – participants compete to see who can stage the most convincing display of despair.

There are canons that feed this framework such as Rachel Carson's *Silent Spring* and Paul Ehrlich's *The Population Bomb*, both of which foretold environmental crises that have not come to pass, but they still feed the network discourse. Vice President Gore's book, *Earth in the Balance* has taken on canonical status, explicitly arguing that scientists who disagree with what Easterbrook calls 'the doomsday premise' are unethical and ought to be ignored.[29] The attitude among environmentalists in the network is that those who disagree are out to 'undermine' or 'subvert' their efforts to save the earth. While environmentalists argue that impending disasters are about to end 'life as we know it', those who oppose this view operate from the other extreme, arguing that environmentalism is a plot to strangle American corporate capitalism.

Journalists who cover environmental policy have naturally spread messages which reflect this discourse and the institutional needs of its inhabitants. Representatives of environmental organizations convinced the editorial staff of the *Cleveland Plain Dealer* to write a piece arguing for the inclusion of an acid rain provision in a proposed bill to amend the Clean Air Act, even though the scientific data were at best unclear, the economic burdens would fall most heavily on the Midwest and the proposal would most likely politically derail the entire bill. These organizations were trying to exert pressure on then Ohio Representative Dennis Eckart who was visibly weighing the arguments on both sides. The editorial was titled 'Sympathy for the Acid Rain Devil' and it argued that the fragility of the environment and impending crises outweighed any 'short-term' economic concerns. Eckart ultimately acquiesced, but the proposed Clean Air Act revisions were rejected.[30]

Thinking of the institutions of the press as facilitators of conversations in policy networks enables analysts to capture the waves in which messages reflect the organization of institutional relations and discourse in the American political system. Are policy networks too amorphous and difficult to define and use as units of analysis? While analysts of any issue area may quarrel around the margins about which groups or individuals 'matter' in any given policy debate, there is generally a fair amount of consensus for any issue area about who the significant participants are at any given moment in time. Admittedly, for some policy networks the number of participants may be quite large and their views and frameworks divergent and time-consuming to catalogue. Robert Salisbury notes that self-interested groups as well as issue organizations or externality groups have proliferated over the last couple of decades overrunning the easily-identifiable, established patterns of the iron triangles of the 1950s. Issues such as health care are no longer dominated by the AMA, but include organizations representing hospital construction interests, medical research, veterans, medical schools, drug companies, senior citizens and a host of others. Think-tanks like the Heritage Foundation and citizens' groups like Common Cause speak out on a wide range of issues on the public agenda – in other words they may jump into just about any policy network.[31] Groups like the Cato Institute and the Competitive Enterprise Institute have launched projects on the environment in order to counter the discourse

Easterbrook describes with another version of extremism. In spite of their size and fluidity, it is possible to 'map' these networks as Salisbury and others have shown.[32] These analyses also suggest that the Washington community has the propensity to be flooded with messages as the number of discussants in many issue areas proliferates. What effect does the press have on the policy-making conversation within networks and beyond to the rest of the Washington community and the American political system? Under what circumstances does the press help policy-makers and others to make sense of numerous and conflicting messages, selecting signals from noise – or are they more likely to mirror the confusion? Does the press ever serve as uniting force for collective action or are they more likely to contribute to the de-stabilization and fragmentation Salisbury describes?

Crafting the Message

In order to answer these questions, we need to look at the ways the press cover the ever-growing and changing cast of participants on their beats. What is news and why is it the way it is? How do the press interpret messages – especially conflicting messages and multiple frameworks? Four categories of explanations appear in most analyses of the press and most serious students believe that in some combination they determine the press' behaviour.

News Organizations and Professional Norms

Many sociologists and political scientists view news as the product of organizational dynamics and professional socialization. That is, news is the unplanned, unintended result of a series of small, routine choices made by reporters and editors as they go about their work. As Leon Sigal found in his study of Washington reporters, journalists' work routines reflect the need to adapt to an uncertain, rapidly changing environment. Work routines enable reporters to simplify events and reassure themselves that they understand what is going on in the world.[33]

So many frequently criticized journalistic habits are exactly that – conventions directly attributable to the way news organizations and reporters make routine choices as they go about their work. 'Pack journalism' is a result of the need reporters have to validate their sense of things with their colleagues and to fend off potential doubt from editors. The need for a 'news peg', a focus on a discrete, immediate, visible event, means that reporters will form stories around visible conflicts. Most stories written by the Washington press corps will focus on prominent public officials because the activities of legitimate office holders are by definition newsworthy. Anything they say is news and does not require further defence as an object of investigation, although reporters might feel compelled to provide some 'balance' to the story by seeking out a quote from another public official who has a different point of view.

While it makes sense to highlight the proposals of accountable government officials with appropriate expertise, the result is that certain policy-makers have an easier time getting their messages across than others (and thus have more opportunities to shape the policy network). Washington's most prominent political reporter, David Broder, worries that many reporters are 'too close' to those in power and that this leads to a certain bias in coverage.[34] The press may 'miss' certain trends by concentrating their efforts on those in power. For example, a number of analysts believe that the Washington press corps did not detect the changes that were about to occur in the US Congress in the 1994 election because they focused their news gathering efforts on the Democratic congressional leadership.[35]

There are also great incentives for savvy policy-makers who by the nature of their positions do not command attention, to conjure up ways of attracting press coverage which may not reflect 'reality', but which enable them to send messages to others. Creating newsworthy events or suggesting alternative interpretations of events (that is, 'spin') which spark reporters' imaginations because they hint at the possibility of a future newsworthy event are frequently-used tactics. The Natural Resources Defense Council held a press conference featuring actress Meryl Streep as an 'expert' on the dangers of the food preservative Alar which attracted coverage by the national media and led to congressional hearings. Third party candidates have released the results of their own opinion polls which suggest that their participation in a Presidential campaign, for example, could throw the election to the House of Representatives. As Cokie Roberts notes, journalists who are by the nature of their business attracted to the idea of an unusual outcome will perpetuate these 'analyses', not because they prefer the ultimate outcome, but because it makes for a 'new' story.[36] Thus, news does not so much reflect some objective notion of truth as it does the work routines and professional norms journalists bring to chronicling the policy network's discourse.[37]

The organizational-professional notes explanation of the news offers a concrete, logical picture of the way news is actually made. According to Michael Schudson, Leon Sigal and a number of journalists themselves, it also handles the problem of 'relative autonomy' well, for it shows that reporters are not so much subject to the explicit directives of publishers and editors as to the implicit guidance of conventions and procedures.[38]

However, this explanation still leaves room for reporters to make individual choices among potential sources on the beat and in the language they use to describe events.

Ideology

Many critics of the press continue to argue that news is the way it is because journalists are liberals. In virtually every attitude survey of the national press corps, reporters reveal themselves to vote overwhelmingly for Democrats and to feel a greater affinity for citizens' groups than business organizations.[39] Austin Ranney puts a finer spin on this pattern – journalists reflect the views of the Progressive movement. They believe in capitalism, the two-party system and the potential for improving society through political reform.[40] Herbert Gans argues that these biases exist because the sorts of individuals who hold these views (people who attended liberal arts colleges, who are upwardly mobile, and who share the views and values of the upper middle class) are recruited to journalism as a profession.[41] What is not clear from either explanation is whether journalists' views are a function of social background or socialization on the job. While it makes sense to look for ways in which the Progressive bias influences story ideas and content, most attempts to do so have merely hinted at effects in story choice and language that could be explained as readily by professional norms and organizational dynamics.

Others argue that it is the ideology of publishers and editors which determines the news. Michael Schudson refers to this explanation as the 'People magazine theory', best exemplified by David Halberstam whose 1970s' account of the major American media is dominated by a handful of powerful figures who define what news is.[42] While powerful media moguls have exercised control in the past, most analysts agree that contemporary journalists operate quite autonomously from owners and publishers and that they are primarily attuned to their peers. Former *Washington Post* publisher Katherine Graham once said that she could not have stopped Woodward and Bernstein and their editors from pursuing the Watergate story even if she had wanted to succumb to White House pressure to do so. The campaign waged from the newsroom to keep following leads as they developed was much more formidable than Presidential threats.[43]

While common sense would suggest that shared ideology might find its way into the news, it is methodologically difficult to demonstrate its independent effects in any consistent way. Above all, the widespread acceptance of the professional norms of journalism means that the personal views of publishers, editors and reporters are unlikely to emerge clearly beyond the editorial and opinion pages.

Culture

As noted above, reporters tend to reflect the culture and the discourse of the networks they cover. Many analysts of the press, argue that reporters also operate within a professional culture based on collectively-adopted frameworks. Most of these interpretations are based on the belief that the media's role in Vietnam and Watergate have had significant effects on news-gathering. These include the extension of the 'credibility gap' to virtually all public officials; the seemingly endless search for scandals, regardless of evidence; and beliefs on the part of both politicians and journalists that the press is capable of single-handedly determining the fate of policies and politicians.[44] There is certainly some evidence that Vietnam in particular increased reporters' scepticism about any statement, figure or document released by a public agency or official while it simultaneously eroded the post-Second World War 'domino theory' of world politics shared by most politicians and journalists. The independent effects of Watergate on how reporters view the world are less clear – many analysts believe that Watergate merely reinforced journalists' interpretations of Vietnam.[45] There is some evidence of a post-Watergate reportorial obsession with the personal traits and backgrounds of politicians in part, David Broder argues, because journalists believed that they had overlooked aspects of Richard Nixon's character and past experiences which might have shed light on his presidency.[46]

Journalists are not immune from the shared frameworks and culture of the Washington community. Reporters pick up views and interpretations of political events and politicians at social functions and in other informal settings around town which naturally make their way into news stories and news gathering. Amateur psychoanalysis of prominent political figures is a hobby shared by reporters and policy-makers alike and it provides a way of framing not only profiles of candidates, but policy discussions as well. Current news analyses of the renewed debate over affirmative action laws are as likely to focus on President Clinton's 'indecisiveness' as they are on the demographic composition of the labour force.[47] Reporters have also been known to pick up the language, opinions, and even the lifestyles and physical appearance of the participants in the policy networks they cover on their beats. Nelson Polsby describes the Washington press corps as 'adrenaline junkies' who are as addicted to the excitement and fast pace of politics as their counterparts at the highest levels of government.

Various attempts at discourse analysis seem to suggest that it is possible to identify some of the ways shared cultural experiences and interpretations make their way into the news – the use of 'Watergate words' such as 'cover-up' in conjunction with any alleged impropriety; the ritual of the 'first hundred days' of a presidency and most recently of the Speaker of the House; and references to world conflicts as 'Vietnams'. The real challenge in these sorts of analyses is to distinguish between alternative 'filing systems' and the effects of organizational dynamics and work routines on news beats.

Markets

Does competition for readers or some other version of the profit motive determine what news is? If we focus on the mainstream newspapers and periodicals which cover government activities in Washington, the answer is no. Subscriptions and daily sales do not come close to covering costs and most national television news shows do not attract ratings which are anywhere near comparable to entertainment programming (including cheap quiz shows). This is not to say that readership surveys and ratings never affect content. Ben Bagdikian argues that the media have been known to protect major advertisers who are the source of the bulk of revenues by, in effect, censoring information that might be harmful to them such as the threats to public health posed by tobacco use. He also suggests that the growth of media conglomerates is leading to news that is heavily weighted in favour of what he refers to as 'corporate values' at the expense of the traditional journalistic norms and values described above.[48] There is certainly some evidence to support Bagdikian's thesis, but there appears to be widespread agreement that it fails to explain more than a small percentage of what appears (or fails to appear) in the mainstream press.

As the number of participants in policy-making has grown in the Washington community, so has what used to be referred to as the 'trade press'; newsletters, magazines and now on-line services which track specific policy networks. These for-profit publications include titles such as *Inside US Trade, Air and Water News,* and on-line services such as *The Hotline.* They command high subscription prices because they are able to provide detailed, specialized information that would not be suitable for publication in widely-circulated dailies. They communicate in the specialized jargon of policy networks. Most of their reporters and writers are not trained or socialized into the journalism profession (they are often former government policy analysts or recent college graduates seeking a launching pad for a future career in policy-making) so stories that do not fit the conventions of standard news reporting often crop up in print – there are no formal or informal requirements for balance; sources are frequently not confirmed; and rumours serve as news pegs.[49]

Is this news? These specialized publications are important vehicles for communication within policy networks. As one interest group

representative said, 'This is the way we talk to each other.'[50] These
publications thrive because policy experts, including journalists, read them.
While one journalist claimed that she takes what these sorts of publications
print 'with a grain of salt', she also admitted to following up on potential
leads triggered by them.[51]

Larry Sabato and others have discussed the ways in which profitable
local television news programmes and radio talk shows have led to
competition for certain types of stories which would not have been tackled
by the Washington press corps in the past.[52] Sabato believes that these sorts
of media personalities contribute to an inappropriate obsession with
rumours and scandals because they lack training and socialization in the
journalism profession. This is a view echoed by David Broder who believes
that news organizations ought to create ways of linking experienced
reporters with those who have just entered the profession.[53]

Decoding the Message

News is a reflection of the messages policy-makers send, the ways in which
the press receive and transmit them and the myriad cultural forces in the
Washington community which shape the conversation in policy networks.
Does this system of news-making and news-gathering serve the American
political system well? If we are concerned with the availability of sheer
volumes of information to both policy-makers and citizens, the press surely
provides it in many forms – from mainstream print, television and radio to
specialized cable television targeted newsletters and on-line services. From
the policy-maker's perspective, there is an ever-growing number of ways to
perpetuate the policy conversation and potentially to shape the policy
network. But there is also considerable competition to do so – a veritable
traffic jam of messages is transmitted, received and processed in a number
of issue areas, reflected in the increased role media strategists play in all
aspects of policy-making. In this sense, one could argue that the press are
contributing to what Salisbury would describe as the fluidity of policy
networks. Multiple and conflicting efforts to shape and re-shape networks
through the press mean that it is going to be very difficult to build coalitions
of more than fleeting endurance.

Viewed from a cultural perspective, this system of policy conversation
is susceptible to individual policy-makers or groups who can conjure up
clever ways to impose frameworks which impose the appearance of order
on the jumble of conflicting messages. Adept participants will find ways to
offer up frameworks that appeal to the press by casting events in a light
which matches the norms, work routines, values and culture of the media in
the Washington community. If the Washington press corps ignore them,

they can send messages through alternative pathways where competition and ideology eclipse the norms of the establishment press. When Washington insiders start to pick up on these alleged events or political assessments, the possibility increases that they will develop resonance in the community and ultimately find their way to the mainstream press. Newt Gringrich's allegations against Jim Wright first appeared in *Regardie's*, a local Washington magazine which attracted little attention from most policy-makers. But Gingrich's persistence in pursuing the story led to a piece in *The Wall Street Journal* which cited the allegations in *Regardie's* and called Jim Wright's ethics into question.[54] Gingrich's efforts fed a point of view that subsequently took hold in the Washington community – that the Democratic leadership was 'out of touch' and 'too complacent'.

The effects of this mode of political conversation are not felt only by politicians facing allegations of scandal, but by citizens as well. The fact that by just about every measure the air and water around us is much cleaner and safer than it was before environmental programmes were implemented over two decades ago is not reflected in public opinion polls where citizens overwhelmingly believe that the environment continues to degrade. Why? Because the press mirror the discourse of the policy network and continue to relate to it 'evidence' in the form of stories about alleged environmental calamities.

The press is frequently criticized for contributing to widespread cynicism among citizens about politicians and government institutions. While Tocqueville and others have noted that these sorts of attitudes are an enduring part of American political culture, there is some evidence to suggest that current trends in the press have exacerbated it. This is not merely a matter of the press's eagerness to unearth scandals. What Larry Sabato refers to as 'feeding frenzies' are not the problem in and of themselves. It is a reflection of the ways in which the media latch on to frameworks and perpetuate modes of discourse that reflect the norms of their profession and the needs and views of their sources in policy networks. As a result, journalists often fail to provide explanations of events that would be useful to citizens who do not know how to decode messages crafted by Washington insiders in collaboration with journalists. Add to this mix the growing number of radio and television talk shows, niche publications and online services which at the very least add to the conflict and often serve to perpetuate misguided frameworks by providing outlets for those whose allegations and interpretations of events would be screened out by the Washington press corps. When Washington insiders embrace these frameworks, as they do on occasion to further political and policy goals, they give the frameworks legitimacy with reporters who must be attuned to the musings of those in power. The result is that ideas and approaches that have little basis in fact become accepted explanations for events throughout the political system. While it would be unreasonable to lay the blame for the Oklahoma City bombing solely at the feet of radio talk show hosts, it is not difficult to see how attitudes could escalate into extremism when citizens and politicians alike are encouraged over the airwaves collectively to lay siege to established political institutions .

In a system in which very few meaningful restrictions are placed on the press, it becomes necessary to rely on politicians' and journalists' own sense of professionalism and civic duty to explain the messages they craft that citizens use to make informed decisions. There is evidence that some are trying to meet high standards. For example, *C-Span*, the cable television network, works hard at giving viewers a sense of the political process seldom provided by other sources. Reconciling the news produced by a free press with the needs of both policy-makers and citizens remains one of the most significant challenges facing the American political system.

NOTES

1. Douglass Cater, *The Fourth Branch of Government* (Boston, MA: Houghton Mifflin, 1959).
2. Ibid., p.7.
3. Bernard Cohen, *The Press and Foreign Policy* (Princeton, NJ: Princeton University Press, 1963). Reprinted in 1993 by the Institute of Governmental Studies Press, University of California, Berkeley.
4. Martin Linsky, *Impact: How the Press Affects Policymaking* (New York: W.W. Norton, 1986).
5. Samuel Kernell, *Going Public: New Strategies of Presidential Leadership* (Washington, DC: CQ Press, 1987).
6. Michael Baruch Grossman and Martha Joynt Kumar, *Portraying the President: The White House and the News Media* (Baltimore, MD: Johns Hopkins University Press, 1980).
7. Elizabeth Drew, *On the Edge: The Clinton Presidency* (New York: Simon & Schuster, 1994). Bob Woodward, *The Agenda: Inside the Clinton White House* (New York: Simon & Schuster, 1994).
8. Kernell, Ch.5.
9. President Clinton's ratings in the polls at the end of 1993, for example, sunk to historic lows for a first-year president.
10. Timothy E. Cook, *Making Laws and Making News* (Washington, DC: Brookings, 1989). Stephen Hess, *Live from Capitol Hill: Studies of Congress and the Media* (Washington, DC: Brookings, 1985). Stephen Hess, *The Ultimate Insiders: U.S. Senators and the National Media* (Washington, DC: Brookings, 1991).
11. Burt Soloman, 'The Editorial We', *National Journal*, 8 Aug. 1986, pp.1881–83.
12. Richard F. Fenno, Jr., *Congress in Committees* (Boston, MA: Little, Brown, 1973).
13. John M. Barry, *The Ambition and the Power* (New York: Penguin Books, 1990).
14. Hugh Heclo, *A Government of Strangers: Executive Politics in Washington* (Washington, DC: Brookings, 1977). Herbert Kaufman, *The Administrative Behavior of Federal Bureau Chiefs* (Washington, DC: Brookings, 1981).
15. Interview with CBS News Correspondent Bob Schieffer, 15 June 1993.
16. Sharon LaFraniere, 'FBI Driver Picked up Director's Wife After Shopping Trip Monday', *The Washington Post*, Saturday, 20 Feb. 1993.
17. Stephen Hess, *The Government Press Connection: Press Officers and Their Offices*

(Washington, DC: Brookings, 1984).

18. Richard Davis, *Decisions and Images: The Supreme Court and the News Media* (Englewood Cliffs, NJ: Prentice Hall, 1994).

19. Timothy E. Cook, 'The Fourth Branch and the Other Three: The Washington News Media and the Politics of Shared Power', paper delivered at the American Political Science Association Annual Meeting, New York, Sept. 1994, pp.30–34.

20. Robert H. Salisbury, 'The Paradox of Interest Groups in Washington – More Groups, Less Clout', Ch.7 in Anthony King (ed.), *The New American Political System* (Washington, DC: American Enterprise Institute, 1978).

21. Hugh Heclo, 'Issue Networks and the Executive Establishment' in Anthony King (ed.), *The New American Political System* (Washington, DC: American Enterprise Institute, 1978) pp.87–124. Peter M. Haas, 'Epistemic Communities and International Policy Coordination', *International Organizations*, Vol.46, No.1., Winter 1992. J. Leiper Freeman, *The Political Process* (New York: Random House, 1965). Douglass Cater, *Power in Washington* (New York: Vintage, 1964).

22. Nelson W. Polsby, 'The Washington Community 1960–1980', in Thomas E. Mann and Norman J. Ornstein (eds.), *The New Congress* (Washington, DC: American Enterprise Institute, 1981).

23. Nelson W. Polsby, 'The Foreign Policy Establishment: Toward Professionalism and Centrism', in Eugene R. Wittkopf (ed.), *Domestic Sources of American Foreign Policy* (New York: St. Martin's Press, 1995).

24. Michael Cornfield, 'The First Hundred Days, 1933–1993: From Historic Event to Media Ritual', unpublished paper, 1994.

25. Michael Schudson, *Discovering the News* (New York: Basic Books, 1978), p.120.

26. Cornfield, pp.9–11.

27. Gregg Easterbrook, *A Moment on the Earth* (New York: Viking , 1995), Preface.

28. Ibid., p. xiii.

29. Ibid., p. xviii.

30. Interview with Graham Dower, *Cleveland Plain Dealer*, 17 June 1989.

31. Salisbury, pp.208–09.

32. John P. Heinz *et al.*, *The Hollow Core: Private Interests in National Policy Making* (Cambridge, MA: Harvard, 1993).

33. Leon V. Sigal, *Reporters and Officials: The Organization and Politics of Newsmaking* (Lexington, MA: D.C. Heath, 1973).

34. David Broder, *Behind the Front Page* (New York: Simon & Schuster, 1987), Ch.9.

35. David Broder, Talk at Stanford in Washington, 24 April 1995.

36. Cokie Roberts, Talk at George Washington University Graduate School of Political Management Forum, 2 June 1995.

37. Edward Jay Epstein, 'Journalism and Truth', *Commentary*, Vol.57 (April 1974), pp.36–40.

38. Sigal, Ch.3. Schudson, pp.117–19.

39. Joseph Keeley, *The Left-Leaning Antenna: Political Bias in Television News* (New Rochelle, NY: Arlington House, 1971). S. Robert Lichter, *et al.*, *The Media Elite: America's New Powerbrokers* (Bethesda, MD: Adler & Adler, 1986).

40. Austin Ranney, 'Broadcasting , Narrowcasting and Politics', in Anthony King (ed.), *The New American Political System* (Washington, DC: American Enterprise Institute, 1978).

41. Herbert J. Gans, *Deciding What's News* (New York: Pantheon, 1979).

42. Schudson, p.115. See also David Halberstam, *The Powers That Be* (New York: Knopf, 1979).

43. Michael Schudson, *Watergate in American Memory* (New York: Basic Books, 1992), pp.105–06.

44. Schudson, *Watergate in American Memory* , Ch.6.

45. Schudson, *Watergate in American Memory* , Ch.6.

46. David Broder, Talk at Stanford in Washington, 24 April 1995.

47. Deborah Adler, 'Affirmative Action: What's in the News', unpublished paper, Stanford in Washington, June 1995.

48. Ben Bagdikian, *The Media Monopoly* (Boston, MA: Beacon Press, 1990).

49. Interview with staff members, *Air and Water News*, 20 June 1989.

50. Interview with Richard Ayers, Natural Resources Defense Council, 17 June 1989.
51. Interview with Rochelle Stanfield, National Journal, 18 June 1989.
52. Larry Sabato, *Feeding Frenzy* (New York: The Free Press, 1993) Ch.2.
53. David Broder, Talk at Stanford in Washington, 24 April 1995.
54. Barry, pp.534–42.

Direct Democracy in California: Example or Warning?

WYN GRANT

This study maintains that the analysis of direct democracy in California can suggest more lessons for students of comparative politics than the traditional Swiss example. The development of direct democracy in California is reviewed and the recent expansion in its use is related to the development of an 'initiatives industry'. As in all aspects of Californian politics, money has a significant impact on the results of referendums. Direct democracy undermines the role of the legislature and encourages politicians to follow popular trends rather than to attempt to exercise political leadership. Various possible reforms of the existing system of direct democracy are reviewed. Although not without its merits, direct democracy in California is more of a warning than an example to be emulated.

The Broader Significance of Californian Experience

Along with other western states such as Oregon and Washington, California is one of the most extensive users of direct democracy in the form of various types of referendum in the United States. Opinion poll evidence suggests that American voters are becoming increasingly disenchanted with the responsiveness of conventional forms of democracy. For example, a Times–Mirror poll conducted in September 1994 of 3,800 adults found that only 33 per cent of the public thinks elected officials care about their beliefs, down from 47 per cent in 1987, while only 42 per cent now believe government is run for the benefit of all the people, compared with 57 per cent in 1987.[1] Do forms of direct democracy offer citizens the chance of overcoming the influence of such inertia reinforcing elements in the polity as incumbency and the role of established interests?

This question has an interest that extends beyond California and the United States. The debate about revitalizing the mechanisms of democratic accountability in a number of countries, not least Britain, has increasingly extended into the area of direct democracy. Traditional defences of the merits of representative democracy have been less secure as the central channel for communication between the people and their elected leaders, the political party, has either atrophied, as in Britain, or fallen apart to be

This study draws on material collected as part of an ESRC funded study on the politics of air quality management in California, reference number L-11925-1001.

replaced by new formations centred around the appeal and financial strength of an individual, as in Italy.

The referendum occurs in democracies in three general forms: (a) referendums instigated by a legislature to approve changes in constitutional arrangements; (b) referendums initiated by a legislature to confirm changes in public policy; (c) citizen initiated measures to change either the constitution or public policy. The first type of measure is relatively common and is used even in countries which generally eschew forms of direct democracy. For example, it has been used in the United Kingdom in relation to devolution in Scotland and Wales, membership of the European Community, and the future status of Northern Ireland. The second type of referendum is less common, while the third is largely confined to the United States. Of the European democracies, only Switzerland makes extensive use of citizen initiative referendums, even more so at the cantonal than the federal level. What happens in Swiss cantons can verge on the quaint, and is of less general interest for students of comparative politics than the western states of the United States. A Swiss canton may have a smaller population than a medium-sized Californian city, and what happens in such small units tells us very little about the possibilities for direct democracy in larger nation states.

Does California offer an example of the way in which traditional forms of democracy might be revitalized, or does it offer a warning about a set of traps to be avoided? A central argument of this article will be that one cannot isolate one aspect of a polity's constitutional arrangements from the other aspects of political structure with which it must necessarily interact. Californian politics has been influenced by the existence of an extensive and increasingly used set of arrangements for direct democracy, but direct democracy in California has been shaped by the particular character of Californian politics. Even a relatively superficial examination of the Californian experience shows the facile character of statements that extending the use of democracy would 'ensure that more decisions are guided by a majority vote rather than by the energies and resources of one pressure group or another'.[2]

The Origins and Forms of Direct Democracy in California

The origins of direct democracy in California date back to the progressive era when the Southern Pacific Railroad lost its grip on the politics of the state and Hiram Johnson, a progressive Republican, was elected as governor in 1910. The initiative, referendum and recall were not, according to Hiram Johnson, 'the panacea for all our ills, yet they do give to the electorate the power of action when desired, and they do place in the hands of the people the means by which they may protect themselves'.[3]

As amended in 1911, the constitution of California provides for the initiative, referendum and recall, while all bond measures also have to be submitted to the voters for their approval. It should be noted that before 1911 the constitution did contain provision for referendums initiated by the legislature. Under Article II, Section 8 (a) of the constitution, 'The initiative is the power of the electors to propose statutes and amendments to the Constitution and to adopt or reject them'. Initiatives are qualified through a petition signed by at least as many electors as five per cent of those who voted at the last election for governor, a figure that increases to eight per cent in the case of amendments to the constitution. Following the 1990 election for governor, the required figures were 384,793 for a statutory initiative and 615,957 for a constitutional amendment.

Not surprisingly, constitutional amendments are less frequently used by the people than initiative statutes. Nevertheless, constitutional amendments are less open to judicial scrutiny because they are normally reviewed only in terms of conformity to the federal constitution. 'That is why, despite more stringent filing requirements, certain initiatives still go the constitutional route'.[4] The legislature can itself place a constitutional amendment on the ballot by a two-thirds vote of the members of each house. From 1884 to the early 1990s, 445 of 685 amendments proposed by the legislature have been adopted, compared with 35 initiative amendments out of a total of 115 proposed.[5] Constitutional amendments proposed by the legislature or the citizens often deal with matters that are substantive rather than procedural. For example, in June 1994 the legislature unsuccessfully attempted to enshrine the renter's tax credit in the constitution. The Marine Resources Protection Act added to the constitution by a citizens' initiative in 1990 is a detailed piece of substantive legislation.

The referendum refers to the power of the electors under Article II, Section 9, to approve or reject statutes or parts of statutes, although not those designated as 'urgency' measures by a two-thirds vote of the legislature. Once again, the qualifying requirement is the signature of at least five per cent of the number of electors voted in the last gubernatorial election. These signatures have to be gathered within 90 days of the enactment of the statute. The referendum is used much less often than the initiative. 'Since its inception, only thirty-nine ... voter-initiated referendum petitions have qualified for inclusion on the ballot, and only six of these measures have reached the voters since 1940'.[6] The last occasion on which legislative measures have been defeated in a referendum was in 1982 when measures on reapportionment and water were overturned. Since 1966 the legislature has been a professional body, no longer meeting biannually (except for budget approval), but effectively in as continuous a session as any other significant legislature. There are many opportunities to influence the legislative process other than through the blunt instrument of a referendum.

Because of its budgetary difficulties the state has increasingly resorted to the issue of bonds as a funding device. What is known as a 'general obligation bond' (in effect, one that is not a revenue bond where rents or other earnings are generated to repay the bond) must be approved by the electors under Article XVI, Section 2 of the state constitution. In recent years, electors have been increasingly inclined to vote 'no' on bond issues. The three bonds on the ballot in June 1994 were on the relatively popular topics of earthquake relief and repair, school construction and renovation and higher education, but all three were defeated.

The power of recall was also added to the constitution in 1911. Under Article II, Section 14 of the constitution, a petition to recall a statewide officer must be signed by electors equal in number to 12 per cent of the last vote for that office, with signatures from each of five counties equal in number to one per cent of the last vote for the office in that county. For a member of the legislature and judges of courts of appeal and trial courts, the number of signatures must equal in number 20 per cent of the last vote for the office.

The recall process has been used mostly at the local level where local governments may adopt their own recall procedures within limits set by state law. San Jose recently experienced its first recall in the city's history when 59.2 per cent of voters approved the recall of an African American council member after she made derogatory comments about Asians, Latinos and gays at a motivational seminar for African Americans. This was a rather exceptional case, but there have been three cases in 1993 and 1994 where cities (Covina, Fullerton and Lincoln) lost a majority of their council members in disputes over new utility taxes imposed in an attempt to deal with chronic budget deficits. The deposed mayor of Fullerton, A.B. 'Buck' Catlin, complained, 'Right now, you can get a recall election just by standing in front of a supermarket telling people to sign this petition if you're against taxes. It's the word "taxes" that acts as the lightning rod'.[7]

The rare attempts to unseat a legislator can have a damaging effect on a political career. David Roberti, at the time the president pro tem of the California Senate, faced a recall election in April 1994 after 46,000 signatures had been collected by a group calling itself the Coalition to Restore Government Integrity, in fact, a front for the gun lobby. Roberti was one of the prime movers behind California's Assault Weapons Control Act of 1989. 'Roberti staved off the recall, but the effort drained his resources and left him with virtually no campaign fund for the Democratic primary for Treasurer in June'. Faced with false attacks by his opponent, 'Roberti, bereft of money, could not respond, and he lost the primary'.[8]

The constitution provides for the exercise of initiative and referendum powers by the electors of each city or county. These powers are extensively used, and having voted on a long list of statewide measures, electors may be confronted by an equally long or even longer list of local measures on which they have to decide. For example, in November 1993, San Francisco voters were given the opportunity to vote on 35 proposals on which they were guided by a 236-page ballot book. In part, this proliferation of measures reflects San Francisco's 'hyperpluralism'. The city charter places strict limits on the actions that may be taken by the Board of Supervisors without voter approval.

The qualifying number of signatures for a proposal in San Francisco in 1993 was 9,964. 16,000 voters supported a ballot on Measure BB which asked whether it 'shall be the policy of the people of San Francisco to allow Police Officer Bob Geary to decide when he may use his puppet Brendan O'Smarty when on duty?'. The police officer's use of his skills as a ventriloquist had been tolerated for some time until he walked into a police breakfast and distracted attention from the speech of the deputy chief. Chief Antony Ribera complained that the practice of using the puppet was detrimental to the good order and efficiency of a paramilitary enforcement agency, but the voters sided with Officer O'Geary by 65,768 to 63,112.

The use of direct democracy in the city does have a more serious purpose. In his study of San Francisco politics, deLeon argues that

> the slow-growth movement was organized almost entirely around initiative campaigns, and it is hard to imagine how that movement could have succeeded without them. The citizen ballot initiative is especially well suited to the city's growing population of highly educated middle-class professionals who tend to be 'elite directing' rather than 'elite directed'.[9]

The Increasing Use of Direct Democracy

'The number of initiatives filed has nearly doubled each decade from the 1950s to the 1990s. More initiatives have been filed in a single year, 1990, than in entire decades from the 1910s through the 1960s.'[10] There is, of course, an important distinction between filing an initiative and seeing it succeed. It is no surprise, for example, that a 1994 initiative on the dignity of the human form, sponsored by Eurica California [sic] of Los Angeles, failed to qualify. This would have provided that 'public exposure of the human breast or chest by men or women be regulated only according to reasonable circumstances'.[11]

If one examines a graph of ballot initiatives, the number circulated starts to rise in the 1960s, and then shows a strong upward trend, albeit with downturns in particular years, through the 1970s and 1980s. The number qualified does not rise as quickly, however, and a wide gap opens up between the number circulated and the number approved. The gap between those qualifying and those approved is narrower. For example, in the years between 1980 and 1990 inclusive, 333 initiatives were circulated, of which 65 (just under 20 per cent) qualified. Of those that qualified, 28 (or over 40 per cent) were successful.

1990 was a record year, with 17 initiatives on the primary ballot in June and 28 propositions on the November ballot (including bond measures). In November four of the 14 bond measures succeeded, but only two of the initiatives, a major one on term limits and one on gill nets sponsored by sport fishing interests. In June 1992, there were just three bond measures on the ballot and no initiatives for the first time since June 1964. In November 1992, the number of ballot measures fell back to 13, of which eight were defeated. The June 1994 contained nine propositions, but only one of these was an initiative placed on the ballot through the signature gathering process: the bulk of the measures were initiated by the legislature or Governor Wilson. The number of ballot measures in November 1994 continued the downward trend from 1990 with five initiatives, a constitutional amendment sponsored by the legislature and a bond measure.

How can one explain the increasing resort to the initiative and other forms of direct democracy? It is important to realize that there is now a significant and highly professional initiatives 'industry' made up of firms which earn all, or a substantial portion, of their income from the management of initiative campaigns. The collection of initiative signatures no longer follows an idyllic pattern of setting up tables on the sidewalk and having a rational discussion with voters before obtaining their signatures. Indeed, those who follow this route may face problems as opposing groups may use blocking tactics. Supporters of an initiative for mobile home rent control found themselves opposed by the Golden State Mobile Home Owners League who 'spend the day telling anyone who walks up to the table that the initiative is a fraud'.[12]

The professional firms make use of paid signature gatherers who receive an agreed fee per name (perhaps a quarter or 35 cents) and mail shots. The two leading firms are Kimball Petition Management of Los Angeles and American Petition Consultants of Sacramento. 'Between 1982 and 1992 nearly 75 per cent (48 of 65) of all of the initiatives on the California ballot have qualified through the efforts of one or other of these two companies. Once hired, they virtually guarantee their clients' ballot status (each has a nearly 100 per cent success rate)'.[13] They work through independent petition subcontractors, securing economies of scale by having packages of initiatives to offer. In order to thrive, companies like these have to stimulate the initiatives market, and may sometimes search out issues which seem to offer the prospect of a good return:

> If some entrepreneur in the business of politics and direct-mail believes that [a] citizen's idea for an initiative would appeal to some particular group (political conservatives, for instance), then the entrepreneur may finance a test mailing ... Eventually, the citizen's initiative will qualify for the ballot and the entrepreneur – through fees, commissions and charges – will have made a nice bundle.[14]

The growth of direct democracy cannot, however, be explained simply in terms of the need for professional campaign management firms to sustain the market. The success of the tax cutting Proposition 13 in 1978 boosted awareness that direct democracy could be used to initiate major changes in policy. There has been a growing trend to attempt to confuse the electors by running counter initiatives, so that the environmental 'big green' initiative in 1990 was countered by 'big brown' sponsored by business interests. There has also been an increasing tendency for members of the legislature to back or even sponsor initiatives as part of their re-election strategies. 'Since 1978 Republican incumbents have proposed twice as many initiatives as Democrats'.[15] In part, this is because they offer an alternative means of achieving policy objectives which have often been frustrated in a Democratic controlled legislature. They can also define election agendas in a way which undermine Democratic candidates as happened with Proposition 187 in the 1994 elections for governor.

Support for the initiative among California voters has fallen off from 83 per cent in 1979 to 66 per cent in the early 1990s.[16] That still represents a very considerable level of support, although the proliferation of initiatives in 1990 did lead to some signs of voter fatigue. There has been some discussion of initiative reform, although this forms part of a wider debate about constitutional reform, which in turn reflects a broader discontent about the unsatisfactory functioning of the democratic process.

Direct Democracy: An Assessment

The original intention of the Progressive reformers was to take power away from vested interests, represented in their day by the Southern Pacific Railroad, and restore it to the ordinary citizen. No doubt there are citizens who carefully read the arguments for and against each proposition, and the accompanying commentary of the legislative analyst, set out in the California ballot pamphlet. It would, however, be an irrational use of the time of each voter to carefully evaluate how she should vote on each proposition. Voters may be influenced by television adverts in which well-known actors advise them to vote yes or no on this or that proposition. They may clip a voting guide out of their newspaper or follow the advice of a pressure group, or they may simply vote 'no' out of cussedness.

The Influence of Money

The conduct of politics is an expensive business. The average tab for winning a seat in the state legislature is calculated to be at least $350,000 in the Assembly and $750,000 for the Senate. While some propositions may attract very little spending on either side, nearly $20 million had been spent by mid-October 1994 on the five major initiatives on the November ballot. The most lopsided spending campaign was over Proposition 184, the 'three strikes and you're out' measure where supporters spent nearly a million dollars and opponents just $9,000 (the measure was passed by 72 per cent to 28 per cent).[17] Even at a local level, large sums of money may be spent. In 1993, a measure to impose rent controls on mobile home parks in Sacramento County was opposed by the park owners who spent $700,000 against $8,000 raised by the supporters of Proposition P.[18] Not surprisingly, the measure was defeated.

Evidence from local ballots suggests that 'greater campaign spending seems to be strongly related to the likelihood of electoral success, regardless of whether the spending is in favor of or opposed to the measure ... for every 1 per cent increase in the proportion of pro-ballot spending, there was a .15 percent increase in the proportion of pro-ballot measure vote'.[19] (See Table 1.) At the state level, a study of initiative campaigns in the 1976-86 period found that 80 per cent of the campaigns had either one-side positive (averaging at $2.5 million) or one-sided negative (averaging at $3 million) campaigning. 'Of the thirteen campaigns with one-sided negative spending, only one passed, while of the six campaigns characterized by rough parity in spending, the pass-fail ratio was an even 50–50. Nine of the thirteen one-sided positive spending campaigns were successful.[20] As voters have become more sceptical about any proposition, the general pattern in the 1990s at state level has been summarized as follows:

> For initiative campaigns in general, high spending on the 'No' side almost always results in a 'No' vote. High spending on both sides also tends to result in a 'No' vote. Even high spending on the 'Yes' side is no guarantee of victory – the tobacco companies spent $60 million on Prop. 188 and still lost by a 2-1 margin.[21]

As the case of Proposition 188 in 1994 shows, voters do have enough knowledge and judgement to detect attempts by business interests to use the initiative process to serve their own interests. This initiative was backed by

TABLE 1
RELATIONSHIP OF CAMPAIGN SPENDING TO BALLOT MEASURE
OUTCOME IN CALIFORNIAN CITIES, 1983–88

	Opponents Outspent Proponents	Proponents Outspent Opponents
Measure Won	35% (13)	68% (19)
Measure Lost	65% (27)	32% (9)

Note: Adapted from data reported by David Hadwiger in *Public Affairs Report*, Vol.33, No.4 (July 1992).

Philip Morris and other tobacco interests. 'At an estimated $6 a signature, the campaign is reckoned to be the costliest ballot initiative ever launched in California'.[22] Philip Morris alone contributed $12.5 million to the campaign, the single largest donation ever. The measure would have replaced tough local measures on smoking by a more limited statewide smoking ban that would have permitted smoking in most public places. The supporters of the measure emphasized its more positive features such as increasing fines for selling tobacco to minors. Towards the end of the campaign, the American Medical Association and various voluntary health organizations found enough money to fund radio spots featuring a former Surgeon General which put across the simple message that the proposition was sponsored by the tobacco companies. This was enough information for the voters who defeated the measure by a 70 per cent to 30 per cent margin.

It should not be assumed that supporters of the more conservative position on a ballot necessarily have more funds. In the November 1993 vote on Proposition 174 on education vouchers, the yes side mustered $3,682,329. The California Republican Party donated $419,309, while the Christian Coalition came up with $130,000. They were easily outspent by the opponents of the measure who came up with $23,954,201, of which $12.4 million came from the influential California Teachers Association.[23] The measure was defeated by a seventy per cent to thirty per cent margin, although it should be noted that the fact that it came to be seen as badly drafted contributed to the outcome.

Some cause groups make considerable use of the initiative process, notably the Planning and Conservation League (PCL), an environmental organization. Even if the initiatives do not succeed they are seen as a worthwhile tactic in terms of mobilizing and maintaining member support, as a PCL official explained in interview:

Respondent: If it's successful like Proposition 166 was, it's extremely important, but if they fail it seems to pretty much go unnoticed and people forget about it very quickly and so it's not so much of a damaging

thing if it doesn't go through ... it's almost as if we're anonymous until
it gets passed, and then we'll use all the publicity we can.

WG: But if it fails, it doesn't damage you?

Respondent: Right. A lot of people would look at, well at least they
gave it a shot, they gave it a try, let's commend them for that.[24]

Following the heavy defeat of Proposition 185 in November 1994, with
no one county voting in favour, the same official admitted, 'These are
discouraging numbers indeed for transit activists, numbers which indicate
that perhaps the initiative process is no longer a reliable method to bring
progress to California's struggling public transportation systems'.[25]
Moreover, the PCL have been criticized for aligning themselves with
business interests in order to obtain funds for their campaigns. Ironically,
given that the initiative process was originally introduced to reduce the
influence of the Southern Pacific Railroad, the PCL was criticized by
legislators for taking support from the railroad to back its campaign on
Proposition 185. Southern Pacific would have gained $1 billion by selling
rights of way if the measure had passed, so its donation of $449,000 in cash
and services to the campaign is not surprising.

Even if a measure its passed, its implementation may be delayed or even
frustrated altogether by subsequent action in the courts. Proposition 187 on
illegal immigration was tied up in a number of court actions immediately it
passed, although the executive branch declared its intention to put as much of
it into effect as possible. In 1988, the electors passed two campaign reform
initiatives, Proposition 68 and 73. Proposition 73 was declared unconstitu-
tional, ultimately by the 9th Circuit Court of Appeals, on the grounds that, as
written, its contributions provision discriminated in favour of incumbents. The
California Supreme Court ruled that even though Proposition 73 was dead it
cancelled Proposition 68 by obtaining five per cent more votes. In 1994, six
years after the original vote, the state court ruled that it would consider a plea
to repair Proposition 73 and put it into effect, although such a decision would
set up a conflict between the federal and state courts. The general point is that,
given the American propensity to resort to the courts, litigation about an
initiative can continue for years after it was passed.

The Impact on the Political Process

Critics of direct democracy in California argue that it has a debilitating
effect on the role of the legislature, although it is open to question whether
the shortcomings of the legislature encourage a resort to the initiative, rather
than the use of direct democracy undermining an august and efficient
institution. The events that occurred following a deadlocked result after the

1994 Assembly elections were hardly those of a dignified and well managed body, including the unsatisfactorily explained hospitalization of the presiding clerk, and a decision by the Republican delegation to remove themselves from the chamber to the Hyatt hotel. One former member of the Assembly has argued that 'too many initiatives end up on the ballot because of the "debilitating" partisan bickering that characterizes the Assembly'.[26]

The existence of direct democracy does have the effect of undermining the authority of the legislature. Members of the legislature may decide to appeal direct to the voters themselves, while lobbyists may hint at the possibility of an initiative campaign if legislation does not go their way. Proposition 13 in 1978 passed despite the opposition of many politicians to it, making them scared of taking a similar stand in future. Part of the argument against initiatives is that their availability can discourage politicians from exercising leadership, encouraging them rather to let events decide matters. The opportunistic politician can jump on the bandwagon of a particular initiative once it proves to be popular. Just such a manoeuvre in relation to Proposition 187 on illegal immigration helped to define and give momentum to the re-election campaign of Governor Pete Wilson in 1994.

Perhaps some of the most serious effects have been on the legislature's ability to fix the state's budget which in many ways is its most important and difficult task. The 'budget by initiative' trend has made it more difficult for the governor and state officials to increase revenues or make effective cuts in expenditure. Proposition 13 seriously increased pressures on the state budget because a higher proportion of local government expenditure had to be funded in Sacramento. 'Once the policy decision was made to replace the lost local revenues with state funds, the local assistance portion of the state budget increased dramatically'.[27] Two initiatives in 1982 modified the state's gift and inheritance tax and indexed personal income tax ranges in line with inflation. The effect of these measures 'was to further reduce the state's tax base and provide additional constraints on the budget'.[28]

On the expenditure side in 1988 voters passed Proposition 98 which guaranteed at least 40 per cent of all general revenue tax for educational purposes. Although this provided an initial boost for educational spending, 'Sagging tax revenues and the massive 1991 and 1992 budget deficits effectively neutralized the impact of Proposition 98'.[29] The 40 per cent figure started to operate as a maximum rather than minimum, failing to generate enough money to cope with the problems of an education system facing a very diverse clientele. This offers a further illustration of the way in which an initiative vote can have outcomes very different from those which the supporters of the measure intended.

Reform of Direct Democracy

Concern about the functioning of direct democracy in California has led to a number of proposals for reform. Lee sets forward an interesting menu of proposed reforms.[30] Some of these are limited but sensible suggestions, such as making the sponsorship of initiatives clear on the petition itself; identifying the major financial supporters in the ballot pamphlet; and restricting the initiative to the November ballot, as used to be the case until 1970, to ensure a more representative vote. The idea of a pre-petition review by a qualified agency to improve the technical quality of proposals is an interesting one, but it is not clear how this agency would function or what it would do if its advice was rejected. Voters are also unlikely to support any reform which requires additional budgetary expenditure. The effectiveness of public hearings on each initiative would depend on whether they attracted media coverage. Television coverage of state politics in California is increasingly poor, while serious newspaper coverage, although often of a very high quality, is read by a limited number of politically interested individuals.

Lee's more radical proposals proceed from his assumption that there is a need to 'salvage a badly flawed institution'.[31] His proposal that the requirements for constitutional amendements should be made more stringent is well founded, given that the constitution is increasingly cluttered up with measures which have no place in a document that should be concerned with procedures and processes rather than substantive issues. Allowing the legislature to repeal statutory initiatives after a specified period would remove much of the effectiveness of direct democracy and would only be desirable if one accepts Lee's argument that 'Despite the enormity of the impact of the initiative process on California's political life, it is doubtful that the resulting product has been worth the candle'.[32] His proposal that there should be a minimum turnout threshold of, say, 50 per cent has some merit, but pursued to its logical conclusion it would disqualify most aspects of the democratic process in California.

A thorough review of the initiative process by the California Policy Seminar of the University of California emphasizes that 'California should specifically acknowledge the differences between the initiative and the legislative process, rather than assuming that the governing principles should be the same'.[33] The constitution currently prescribes that 'An initiative measure embracing more than one subject may not be submitted to the electors or have any effect'. This single subject rule 'has given rise to a good deal of litigation but has proved to be a toothless tiger'.[34] The California Policy Seminar document recommends that California should adopt a new rule for initiatives that defines single subject more narrowly than hitherto.

More controversially, it is argued that there should be no more than six statewide initiatives on any single ballot, selected in their order of qualification. This would deal with one of the principal objections of electors to the process as it operates at the moment, that there are simply too many measures on the ballot. However, as those left over would be placed on the next ballot, a queue would quickly develop. Moreover, most of the items on the statewide ballot are usually placed there by the legislature, so its measures would be favoured relative to those coming from the people. The measures likely to qualify first would be those backed by well-financed interests able to afford speedy signature collection drives.

A Citizen's Commission on Ballot Initiatives was set up in the 1991–92 legislative session and issued its report in January 1994. Their principal proposal was the restoration of a modified 'indirect' initiative under which qualified measures would go to the legislature for evaluation. Hearings would be held, and sponsors could accept amendments to iron out flaws in the proposal, provided that they were consistent with the original objectives. The measure could be voted into law by the legislature without going to the electorate. There is much to be said for this proposal, although it would represent a break with the original philosophy of direct democracy in California by inserting the legislature into the process. In practice, however, the legislature is in the process anyway because so many legislators are involved in sponsoring initiatives. This proposal would enable flaws in measures to be removed and it should have the effect of reducing the number of measures appearing on the ballot.

The Limits of Direct Democracy

Lee argues that representative government is threatened by the initiative process itself.

> In a paradoxical turn of events, the initiative, instead of serving as a safety valve, has become an uncontrolled political force of its own. It is a force that has produced occasional benefits but at an extraordinary cost – an erosion of responsibility in the executive and legislative branches of state government, a simultaneous overload in the judiciary, and an excessively amended state constitution alongside a body of inflexible quasi-constitutional statutory law.[35]

This perspective places too much of the burden for the flaws of the governing process in California on one element of it, direct democracy.

The failures of the governing process have to be placed in the context of the problems that the state faces. The end of the cold war undermined the defence industry and defence bases on which much of the state's economy was founded. The aerospace industry alone has lost 150,000 jobs since 1986, and is expected to lose another 80,000 by the end of the decade. Aerospace industry jobs have been well paid and had a significant multiplier effect in the local economy. Aerospace firms have had a good record of employing members of ethnic minority groups. A substantial gap opened up in California and national employment rates in the recession of the early 1990s. For example, in October 1993, the unemployment rate in California was 9.8 per cent compared with 6.8 per cent for the United States. The average gap in 1994 is expected to be nearly four per cent.[36]

The economic downturn has exacerbated the state's budgetary problems at a time when it faces unavoidable increased expenditure on prisons to cope with the consequences of 'three strikes and you're out' legislation. As noted earlier, initiatives have constrained the options open to the executive and legislature in constructing the state budget. However, the two-thirds vote required for appropriations measures in the legislature is a more significant constraint.

Underlying the state's budgetary problems are the tensions created by its ethnic diversity. Eighty-two languages are taught in the Los Angeles Unified School District.[37] Anglos now constitute 57 per cent of the state's population, but they normally account for over 80 per cent of voters. Although African Americans have long been entrenched in the state legislature, and Latinos and Latinas are increasingly represented (partly as a result of redistricting), the political process in California is dominated by high income whites. Many of these whites, who increasingly live in guarded gated communities, have little interest in spending on public schools which they do not use for their children, or on welfare which they perceive as benefiting illegal immigrants. The size of the gulf between the well-off white (and Asian American) middle class and and the under class is a large one in economic and political terms: the middle class of well-paid manual workers has shrunk substantially in size. 'The most likely political scenario for California in the 1990s and at least the early years of the 21st century is for dominance by an affluent, politically active overclass using its position to protect its privileges against the larger but weaker underclass.[38] Direct democracy does not mean a lot if you live in a drug-infested neighbourhood in south central Los Angeles plagued by drive-by shootings, but then it probably does not mean a lot to up-scale individuals living in Marin County and commuting by ferry to a well-paid job in the San Francisco financial district.

As Cronin observes, 'most of the perceived flaws of the direct democracy process are the flaws of democracy in general'.[39] In California, the whole democratic process is permeated by the importance of money in

securing desired political outcomes, and the influence of the special
interests that provide the money. There are, however, limits to money's
influence. You cannot buy an election, as Michael Huffington discovered,
and voters can see through moves by special interests like the 1994 initiative
backed by the major tobacco companies. Proposition 187 on illegal
immigration may not reflect well on the liberal sentiments of California
voters, but some voters justified their support on the grounds that the courts
would stop the proposition being implemented, but it would send a message
to the federal government about the seriousness of the illegal immigration
problem. The initiative can be a useful safety valve.

'Direct democracy devices occasionally permit those who are motivated
and interested in public policy issues to have a direct personal input by
recording their vote, but this is a long way from claiming that direct
democracy gives a significant voice to ordinary citizens on a regular
basis'.[40] If direct democracy placed Californians in control of their political
process, they would presumably not have found it necessary to introduce
term limits for legislators, but the initiative process gave them the
opportunity to make what has proved to be a major change in the rules of
the political game. Given support for direct democracy by a diverse
coalition of interests ranging from conservative Republicans to
environmentalists, it is likely to remain a feature of the political process in
California. Some reform is desirable, but is likely to be difficult to achieve
given the considerable elements of inertia in the political process.

Even with modern methods of communication, distance lends
enchantment, and rather idealized accounts of direct democracy in
California appear in the quality press in Britain as part of the debate about
constitutional reform. Direct democracy in California represents an
imperfect addition to a flawed political process. The vision of the
progressive Republicans was one which saw it as possible to bring the
political process under the control of the people to achieve desired social
reforms. Even in the 1920s, however, the initiative process was used by the
kingpin lobbyist of the day, Artie Samish, to achieve the ends of his clients.

The contemporary United States suffers from a deep political malaise.
At a time when the economy is performing far better than many of the
gloomy forecasts of the 1980s anticipated, voters are deeply disillusioned
with politicians and the political process. In part, this reflects the intractable
social problem represented by an entrenched under class and the associated
problems of substance abuse and crime. Issues such as abortion, which
divide Americans deeply, could never be satisfactorily resolved by a
referendum process which would only further polarize the opposed camps.
There has been a loss of faith in the capacity of government to solve social
problems. Direct democracy could not restore that faith, nor does it provide

a satisfactory means for solving complex social problems.

The end of the California dream is a recurrent theme of contemporary commentaries on the golden state. From a British perspective, the state still offers a rather good lifestyle, and even experienced commentators from inside the state may find much to commend in the political aspects of the Californian good life. One experienced writer on Californian politics has observed, 'California is blessed with participatory democracy of a very high level'.[41] It is also blessed with a highly educated political class that is open and receptive to new ideas. Political tourists to California might be better advised to focus on the open and systematic discussion of policy options than on bringing back ideas about direct democracy with their intellectual baggage. Direct democracy in California should be regarded more as a warning than as an example.

NOTES

1. *Sacramento Bee*, 21 Sept. 1994.
2. *The Economist*, 29 Oct. 1994.
3. Quoted in Eugene C. Lee and L.L. Berg, *The Challenge of California*, 2nd edn. (Boston, MA: Little, Brown, 1976), p.98.
4. Richard B. Harvey, *The Dynamics of California Government and Politics*, 4th edn. (Dubuque, IA: Kendall-Hunt, 1991), p.67.
5. League of Women Voters of California, *Guide to California Government*, 14th edn. (Sacramento, CA: League of Women Voters), pp.3–4
6. James W. Lamare, *California Politics: Economics, Power and Policy* (St. Paul, MN: West Publishing, 1994), p.57.
7. *Sacramento Bee*, 30 June 1994.
8. A.G. Block, 'David Roberti', *California Journal*, Vol.25, No.11 (1994), pp.9–11, p.9
9. Richard E. DeLeon, Progressive Politics in San Francisco 1975–1991 (Lawrence, KS: Kansas University Press, 1992), p.24.
10. Charles Price and Robert Waste, 'Initiatives: Too Much of a Good Thing?', *California Journal*, Vol.22, No.3 (1991), pp.117–20, p.117.
11. *CJ Weekly*, 26 Sept. 1994.
12. *CJ Weekly*, 25 April 1994.
13. Charles Price, 'Signing for Fun and Profit: The Business of Gathering Petition Signatures', *California Government and Politics Annual*, 1994–5 (Sacramento, CA: California Journal Press), pp.75–7, p.76.
14. Robert Fairbanks and Martin Smith, 'There's Gold in Them Thar Campaigns', *California Government and Politics Annual, 1989–90* (Sacramento, CA: California Journal Press), pp.77–80, p.77.
15. Charles Bell and Charles Price, 'Are Ballot Measures the Magic Ride to Success?', *California Government and Politics Annual*, 1990-1, pp.93–5, p.94.
16. Field Institute poll figures cited in Philip L. Dubois and Floyd F. Feeney, *Improving the California Initiative Process: Options for Change* (Berkeley, California Policy Seminar, 1992), p.8.
17. *Sacramento Bee*, 19 Oct. 1994.
18. *The Sacramento Newsletter*, 8 Nov. 1993.
19. David Hadwiger, 'Campaign Spending and Voter Turnout Can Sway Initiative Outcomes', *Public Affairs Report*, Vol.33, No.4 (1992), p.12.
20. Ibid., p.12.

DIRECT DEMOCRACY IN CALIFORNIA 149

21. Michael Bennett Cline, 'Prop. 185 Defeat: What Next?', *California Rail News*, Vol.10, No.5, pp.1-2, p.2.
22. *The Economist*, 23 April 1994.
23. Figures from 'California's Special Measure Election, 2 Nov. 1993, Ballot Measure Campaign Financing', issued by the Secretary of State, Sacramento, 1994.
24. Author's transcript of recorded interview, Sacramento, 18 Aug. 1994.
25. Cline, p.1.
26. *CJ Weekly*, 29 Aug. 1994.
27. Richard Krolak, *California's Budget Dance: Issues and Process* (Sacramento, CA: California Journal Press, 1990), p.6.
28. Ibid., p.7
29. Lamare, p.205.
30. Eugene C. Lee, 'Representative Government and the Initiative Process', in John J. Kirlin and Donald R. Winkler (eds.), *California Policy Choices: Volume Six* (Los Angeles, University of Southern California School of Public Administration, 1990), pp.227-53, pp.251-2.
31. Ibid., p.251.
32. Ibid., p.249
33. Dubois and Feeney, p.4.
34. Ibid., p.248.
35. Lee, p.448.
36. *Sacramento Bee*, 16 Dec. 1993.
37. David Rieff, *Los Angeles: Capital of the Third World* (New York: Simon & Schuster, 1991), p.134.
38. Dan Walters, *The New California*, 2nd edn. (Sacramento, CA: California Journal Press, 1992), p.20.
39. Thomas E. Cronin, *Direct Democracy: The Politics of Initiative, Referendum and Recall* (Cambridge, MA: Harvard University Press, 1989), p.230.
40. Ibid., p.225.
41. Mary Ellen Leary, 'California Dream in Crisis', *California Journal*, Vol.26, No.1 (1995), pp.53-5, p.53.

Notes on Contributors

Wyn Grant is Professor and Chair of the Department of Politics and International Studies at the University of Warwick.

Adrienne M. Jamieson is Director of Stanford in Washington, Standford University.

Desmond King is Fellow in Politics, St. John's College, Oxford.

Ines C. Molinaro teaches in the Department of Politics and International Studies at the University of Warwick.

George Philip is Reader in Comparative and Latin American Politics at the London School of Economics.

Nelson W. Polsby is Director of the Institute of Governmental Studies at the University of California, Berkeley.

Gordon T. Stewart is Chair of the Department of History, Michigan State University.

Alan Ware is Fellow in Politics, Worcester College, Oxford.

For Product Safety Concerns and Information please contact our EU
representative GPSR@taylorandfrancis.com
Taylor & Francis Verlag GmbH, Kaufingerstraße 24, 80331 München, Germany

www.ingramcontent.com/pod-product-compliance
Lightning Source LLC
Chambersburg PA
CBHW020355270326
41926CB00007B/449

9 780714 642642